HOLL ___ ___DIOS

DISNEY'S ANIMAL KINGDOM THEME PARK

REST OF THE RESORT

INTRODUCTION

During the construction of Disneyland, Walt Disney and his team of artists and designers understood that details and flourishes would heighten the Guest experience. Among those touches was the addition of names painted on the windows of Main Street, U.S.A. honoring people who helped bring Disneyland to life. The tradition has been carried through to Walt Disney World. The names go unnoticed by thousands of Guests every day, but for those who know a bit about the Park's history, the hidden names are a special touch.

Hidden Mickeys are like that, too. They're details that bring another layer of entertainment to the Park. Hidden Mickeys began to appear in the 1980s, and there are plenty of opinions about what makes a true Hidden Mickey. For our purposes, a Hidden Mickey is:

- A three-circle silhouette or outline of Mickey Mouse's head composed of a larger, central circle and smaller circles for ears, attached in the right spots. The ears can also be detached, as long as they're not too far away from the head. However, Mickey's head does not have to be right-side up; it can be upside down or sideways.
- A profile of Mickey Mouse's head.
- A full-body outline or silhouette of Mickey Mouse.
- A full-color drawing or other 3-D model of Mickey Mouse.

True Hidden Mickeys are those that have been intentionally placed in a locale, yet are somewhat hard to find. There are hundreds of *obvious* Mickeys, but you have to work to discover a Hidden Mickey. That said, throughout this book, you will find exceptions—Hidden Mickeys that don't quite fit the criteria but are too good to pass up.

A few other notes: this book does not include a Mickey Mouse seen in shows, parades, and other

What we're NOT counting as a Hidden Mickey:

Foods. (That said, see our exception with several fruits and vegetables at Epcot's The Land pavilion on page 68.)

Shadows (unless it's something a bit more stable, like the Pirates of the Caribbean scene with "Old Bill" and the cat on page 46).

Obvious interior décor. (Although we had to mention the merchandise racks in Mouse Gear on page 74.)

Obvious exterior décor (though we're partial to Disney's Pop Century Resort's Mickey phone on page 228).

Characters other than Mickey Mouse (although we couldn't resist calling out Minnie Mouse at the Seven Dwarfs Mine Train on page 29).

amusements that can be expected to change regularly. Hidden Mickeys should be somewhat permanent. We also made some tough editing calls—both because of the sheer volume and the constant pace of change. As such, you won't find images covering resort room interior décor, the championship golf courses, or the mega update known as Disney Springs (formerly the Downtown Disney shopping area) in this edition. If we're lucky, we'll write an updated and expanded edition someday and include them then!

Of course, any Hidden Mickey can disappear when attractions are refurbished. So, if you can't find a particular one, it may be because it's gone. The good news is that new Hidden Mickeys are added from time to time, so keep your eyes open! This book is organized by area. The names of attractions, shops, and restaurants are listed alphabetically. The first part of each entry gives general information about the location of a Hidden Mickey, while the last lines—in italics—are more specific. So, if you only want a hint, don't read the italicized lines! In closing, we would like to thank the Cast Members here at the Walt Disney World Resort for their help in making the assembly of this guide a magical adventure.

Have fun!

— *Kevin and Susan Neary*

P. S. Keep a sharp eye out for this icon on certain entries, earmarking the hardest-to-spot Hidden Mickeys.

WHO'S THE LEADER OF THE BAND?

The largest Hidden Mickeys are the ones you won't be able to see for yourself . . . unless you're in an airplane! The oldest has been at Disney's Hollywood Studios since the Park's opening on May 1, 1989. Echo Lake forms Mickey's left ear, and painted rooftops form his right. Mickey's eyes, forehead, sideburns, and mouth are formed by color changes in the pavement, and the nose is formed by a grassy oval plot. The Park has greatly evolved since 1989; the addition of Sunset Boulevard—plus the giant "Sorcerer's Apprentice" hat in front of the Chinese Theater—have changed this view over time. But underneath all the overlays, the largest Hidden Mickey remains.

The next was formed by a lake in the middle of the infield at the Walt Disney World Speedway (opposite, top), a one-mile racetrack that has hosted a variety of speed events since its 1995 opening—and became known as the home to the now-defunct Richard Petty Driving Experience in which older Guests could sample driving a real NASCAR race car.

The newest aerial-view Hidden Mickey came in 2006 with the construction of Expedition Everest—Legend of the Forbidden Mountain (opposite, middle). The main circle for Mickey's head is shaped by the footprint of the mountain itself, while the ears are formed by curving coaster tracks. (You'll get a better view from satellite imagery that's available online.)

The last large Mickey, although not quite as grand-scale or hidden as the others, is just too good not to mention: a sand trap fondly known as the "Mouse Trap" at Disney's Magnolia Golf Course (opposite, bottom). This bunker located at the sixth hole (though perhaps best viewed from the ladies tee) is the real thing, too; if the ball gets caught in one of the ears, it's extremely difficult to make par.

MAGIC
KINGDOM
PARK

MAIN STREET, U.S.A.

Marking the gateway to the Magic
Kingdom, Main Street, U.S.A.
transports Guests back to the
turn-of-the-last century, when a
more innocent attitude and happy
mood seemingly prevailed. The
area runs from the Walt Disney
World Railroad Main Street
station and Town Square up to
the hub.

Curtain Call Collectibles: Adjacent to the Town Square Theater, the shop features a collection of Disney-themed goods and hats. Find a sewing machine stand located at the front of the store with a Mary Poppins dress on display.

On the sewing machine is a spool of thread attached to the machine with a Mickey head on the top of the spool.

Curtain Call Collectibles: Farther back in the shop, is a collection of Mickey designs.

There is a Hidden Mickey in the shape of locks on the center fixture inside the shop.

Curtain Call Collectibles: There is also a classic Hidden Mickey on the front of Mickey's house.

It is depicted as a dollhouse on the ledge of the shop above the cash/wrap area of the store.

Emporium: In the newest section of the Emporium, in the back portion of the store that connects with a side street that used to be known as Flower Street, locate a wall mural featuring a turn-of-the-century display of what life was like over a hundred years ago.

A REAL TUFFY *On the far left of this mural is a side profile of a smiling child. Look closely at his ear; inside is a classic Hidden Mickey.*

On that same mural, there is a plaque displaying a date; an upside-down Hidden Mickey lays in the scrollwork of the sign.

Emporium: On a sidewall near the Emporium's entrance closer to Cinderella Castle, there is a display shelf.

Above the display, there is a carved wooden decoration that closely resembles Mickey's head.

Emporium/Main Street Athletic Club: Located between the two shops, find a side street with a closed door displaying two Hidden Mickeys.

One is located at the top and the other is at the bottom in the scrollwork of the glass window.

Emporium/Main Street Confectionery: Merchandise-display poles with the classic Mickey head can be found throughout these two stores.

Additionally, keep a lookout for these types of display poles throughout the Walt Disney World Resort property.

Emporium windows: On the outside of this store's walls are a collection of themed windows that are all inspired by Disney animated features.

In the Aladdin–inspired window, there is a model of the city of Agrabah. Look closely and you may notice a window that is in the shape of a Mickey head.

👉 **Emporium windows:** In another window display, near the end of the shop, there is a collection of turn-of-the-century artifacts, including a piano.

The piano's Hidden Mickey is located above the piano keys in what looks like a pipe organ emblem. Also check out the brand name printed under it: STEINMOUSE & SONS, instead of the famed piano maker Steinway & Sons.

👍 **Main Street Car Barn:** Located next to the Emporium is the Car Barn, home to the horseless carriage transportation system that serves Main Street, U.S.A.

On an inside wall, there's a glass case that features a collection of horse bridles that sport several Hidden Mickey shapes, including those for the top and the sides of the horse's gear. When the horses are out and about on Main Street, U.S.A., they don the same bridles.

👈 **Main Street Confectionery:** For those who have a sweet tooth, this is the place for you. Gear up for a Hidden Mickey in the window.

In one of the outside windows, there are three gears—one large and two smaller devices—that form a classic Hidden Mickey. Also notice the two smaller Hidden Mickeys within the large one's ears.

 Plaza Restaurant: Inside, there is a Hidden Mickey located in one of the pictures on the far right wall of the restaurant.

Look above the old-fashioned picture of a woman and you will discover a classic Hidden Mickey.

A REAL TUFFY **Side street:** Here is a very difficult Hidden Mickey to spot, even for the sharpest, most-trained seekers. As you exit Uptown Jewelers, there is a small side street that divides Main Street, U.S.A.

Look down at the cement, near the curb and along the main street, to glimpse a small Hidden Mickey impression in the cement.

 **Tony's Town Square Restaurant:** The 1955 Disney animated feature *Lady and the Tramp* provides the inspiration for the Main Street, U.S.A. restaurant. Immediately inside the main dining area, locate a shelf directly on the left-hand sidewall.

On the shelf is a flower basket with a grouping of three red flowers strategically forming a classic Hidden Mickey.

 **Tony's Town Square Restaurant:** As you exit the sides of the restaurant, look directly up at the back side of the restaurant's sign.

There you will spot a classic Hidden Mickey in the sign's gold leafing.

👉 **Town Square Theater:** Guests of all ages get their chance to meet and greet Mickey Mouse at this Main Street, U.S.A. location. Once in his room, look for a chest with magic supplies inside.

Mickey, who has always been known to dabble with magic, has three rings in the chest that form a classic image of himself.

👍 **Walt Disney World Railroad station:** The train station above the Park's entry area features a collection of Hidden Mickey designs. The first is situated along the top portion of the train station itself.

The wrought iron gate work has a repeating Mickey head design running along the roof.

 Walt Disney World Railroad station:
Appropriately, there is a symbolic railroad ticket office window located on the side facing Cinderella Castle where searchers can spot two Hidden Mickey designs.

There is a gold-colored lock on the sidewall with a design that resembles Mickey.

 There are a few luggage tags on the counter of the ticket window. An image that looks somewhat like a Mickey head is on the topmost luggage tag.

 Walt Disney World Railroad station: As you exit the train station and make your way down to Main Street, U.S.A., head toward Cinderella Castle. Once on the street, look back toward the train station and on the second floor of the building near the outside patio area.

There are three circles on the underside of the roof. When viewed from just the right angle, they form a classic Hidden Mickey.

FANTASYLAND

For the opening of Disneyland Park, Walt Disney described Fantasyland as, "[A] world of imagination, hopes, and dreams. In this timeless land of enchantment, the age of chivalry, magic, and make-believe are reborn—and fairy tales come true...."

Castle Couture: Throughout this shop's interior, there is beautiful bronze-colored crown molding featuring reliefs of flowering plants. Anything look familiar?

Across from the PhotoPass desk turn to look at the crown molding and then count forward six arches from the left. There you will discover a single flower that resembles a Mickey head.

👉 **"it's a small world":** Considered by many as the "happiest cruise that ever sailed," the boat attraction journeys to a Hidden Mickey in the Africa show scene.

Look among the leaves and the vines for purple leaves that form a classic Hidden Mickey.

👍 **The Many Adventures of Winnie the Pooh:** At the attraction's entrance, see an example of Mr. Sanders's tree house home of Winnie the Pooh. Can you spot the two Hidden Mickey designs inside and the one outside?

The first is on the table, inside the tree house; it's three honey pots that form a classic Hidden Mickey.

The second is etched on the inside of the tree directly above the children's doorway.

The one outside is on the opposite end of the tree's opening, situated behind a fence. A classic Hidden Mickey is etched into the wood on a vertical brown post on the side of the window.

The Many Adventures of Winnie the Pooh:
Always the horticulturist, Rabbit fittingly has his own garden situated in the queue area of the attraction. Let us reveal a Hidden Mickey to you.

There is an assortment of vegetables on a table; take a closer look at a head of lettuce and two tomatoes.

The Many Adventures of Winnie the Pooh:
A little farther along in the queue area are three cut watermelons positioned on a small children's table.

They are actually drums to keep the little ones—and those young at heart—busy while waiting in the line. The three watermelons make for a perfect Hidden Mickey head.

The Many Adventures of Winnie the Pooh:
In one of the early scenes, the Hundred Acre Wood friends are experiencing a very blustery day. Look for the vegetable marker for radishes.

The marker is just to the left of Rabbit. On it, you will discover a perfect tiny Hidden Mickey head.

The Many Adventures of Winnie the Pooh:
In the scene when Pooh falls asleep, look to the wall on your immediate left.

There is a Pooh-Coo Clock with a classic Hidden Mickey on the face of the clock.

👏 **Mickey's PhilharMagic:** All along the back wall of this 3-D spectacular, there is a musical-themed mural.

There are small white Mickey heads scattered throughout the mural among the musical notes and instruments.

👆 **Mickey's PhilharMagic:** Once in the theater, look to the right side of the gold stage.

There is a Hidden Mickey in the French horn.

👍 **Mickey's PhilharMagic:** In the attraction's 3-D film itself, there is a series of Hidden Mickeys.

In the "Be Our Guest" sequence, observe Lumiere closely as he ascends in the air and casts a shadow in the form of Mickey's head.

In The Lion King sequence, look to the far left of the screen; there is a grouping of trees that forms a classic Hidden Mickey.

Last, Tinker Bell's wake of pixie dust forms a perfect Mickey head as she flies toward the clock tower during the Peter Pan sequence.

👏 **Mickey's PhilharMagic gift shop:** Take a look at the top ledge that surrounds this shop. See Mickey standing around?

Along the shop's ceiling ledge are music stands that bear a striking resemblance to Hidden Mickey heads.

👉 **New Fantasyland, The Barnstormer:** Take a look at the large billboard to the right of the attraction's entrance. Anything propel you to look just a little closer?

Find a Hidden Mickey in an airplane on the far right side of the billboard.

👍 **New Fantasyland, The Barnstormer:** Prior to entering the queue area, take a peek at the ticket booth advertising the Great Goofini.

A closer look at the top of the ticket booth, just below Goof's picture, reveals scrollwork shaped like everyone's favorite pal.

A REAL TUFFY **New Fantasyland, Be Our Guest Restaurant:** A classic Hidden Mickey can be found on the short rock wall to the left of the restaurant's check-in desk.

It's on top of the last flat rectangular stone before the wall ends at the left side of the check-in station.

👋 **New Fantasyland, Big Top Souvenirs:** Make your way over to the embroidery station of the merchandise location.

Take a close look at the leg of the cheetah in the picture to spot a classic Hidden Mickey.

👉 **New Fantasyland, Bon Jour! Village Gifts:** Several antique maps that resemble Mickey are featured on the wall inside this shop.

> *Concentrate on the one on your left as you enter the shop, which is listed as the "Terrestrial Globe." It is an upside-down Hidden Mickey.*

👍 **New Fantasyland, Bon Jour! Village Gifts:** Being the avid reader that Belle is, it would only seem appropriate there are extra special bookends in the window of this shop.

> *The bookends in the outside window form the shape of Mickey's head.*

👈 **New Fantasyland, Disney Vacation Club kiosk:** There is a Disney Vacation Club kiosk directly across from the entrance to Under the Sea—Journey of The Little Mermaid.

Look at the globe that marks the entrance to the location, and you will discover a Hidden Mickey in its unique structure. Take note of the smaller Hidden Mickey in the ironwork next to the larger globe.

👉 **New Fantasyland, Dumbo the Flying Elephant:** Look for references to the famous pachyderm throughout Storybook Circus. Anything make an imprint?

> *Look for a collection of hoofprints in the shape of the famous mouse throughout this whimsical land.*

New Fantasyland, the Enchanted Forest grounds: On the footbridge extending from Pinocchio Village Haus to the Enchanted Forest, there are horse hoofprints embedded in the cement walkways.

Find three hoofprints strategically situated together to form a classic Hidden Mickey.

New Fantasyland, the Enchanted Forest grounds: On the same footbridge, look over the wall and down at the water, and you may spot three rocks in the water forming a perfect Mickey head.

If you are standing at Be Our Guest Restaurant, it is on your left side just over the short wall of the bridge.

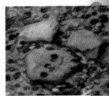

New Fantasyland, Enchanted Tales with Belle: Located above the FastPass+ line, there is a classic Hidden Mickey.

To find it, study the wooden beam prior to entering the attraction.

New Fantasyland, Enchanted Tales with Belle: Inside Maurice's cottage, to the left of the fireplace, is a stack of firewood.

The bottom row of wood, in the very middle, resembles a classic Hidden Mickey design.

A REAL TUFFY New Fantasyland, Gaston's Tavern: You may not be one of Gaston's admirers, but you should still take a look at the mammoth statue that marks the entrance to his eatery. There's a classic Hidden Mickey hollowed out in the rock formation.

Look closely at the base of Gaston's statue, more toward the back end of the structure.

👈 **New Fantasyland, Pete's Silly Sideshow meet and greet:** Look at the front window of the musical calliope manufactured by the Melody Time Brass Horns Co.

Three horns are carefully placed, making for a perfect upside-down Hidden Mickey.

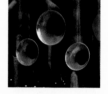

👉 **New Fantasyland, Pete's Silly Sideshow meet and greet:** There is a poster featuring Daisy looking deeply into a crystal ball with multiple Hidden Mickeys.

On Daisy's gypsy-themed shirt, there is a collection of Mickey shapes. There is also a Hidden Mickey in the green mist of the crystal ball.

👍 **New Fantasyland, Seven Dwarfs Mine Train:** You will have to look closely to discover some truly fantastic Hidden Mickeys scattered throughout this exciting attraction.

A REAL TUFFY *When you are in the queue area waiting to board, embedded on the wall across and above the first row is a classic Mickey head on the wall.*

To the right of Dopey's ears and to the right of the moving vehicle is a Hidden Mickey fashioned

in the many jewels of the dwarfs' diamond mine.

Next, look to your right to discover the lovable Grumpy. On the wall behind him are three jewels on the back wall that form a classic Hidden Mickey.

Your journey continues as you ascend up the side of the mountain. Look quickly to your right once you reach the top of the mountain. There is a miner-themed Hidden Mickey.

A REAL TUFFY *At the end, where Guests disembark, there is a small Minnie plush situated in the crossbeam above the track.*

New Fantasyland, Storybook Circus grounds: On the very back wall of Storybook Circus, there is a tent featuring a large mural depicting the whimsical overview of the themed land.

Look for a collection of Mickey head balloons in the picture. On the side of the restrooms in Storybook Circus, there is another smaller version of the image featuring the same collection of Mickey head balloons.

☞ **New Fantasyland, Under the Sea—Journey of The Little Mermaid:** When you're walking in the standby line on the first bridge, look down and on your right to find this classic Hidden Mickey.

This shape is right on the edge, where the water falls down.

☞ **New Fantasyland, Under the Sea—Journey of The Little Mermaid:** In the queue, look for this classic Hidden Mickey in the rock.

The Hidden Mickey is sideways along the left side.

☞ **New Fantasyland, Under the Sea—Journey of The Little Mermaid:** On the right side along the outside standby entrance, a classic Hidden Mickey makes quite an impression.

Find the imprint at the top right side of a rock that sits in the middle of the small lagoon in front of the waterfall.

☞ **New Fantasyland, Under the Sea—Journey of The Little Mermaid:** Along the right side of the outside queue, look to the right of the small lagoon and high up on the rock hill to locate this beautifully proportioned classic Hidden Mickey impression in the rock's surface.

It's above and left of a crevice and near the top of the rock wall, just to the right of the edge of the large opening into the cavern inside the queue.

☞ **New Fantasyland, Under the Sea—Journey of The Little Mermaid:** When entering the scene where Sebastian is singing "Under the Sea," there are several sets of three purple corals that form a Mickey head.

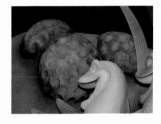

Two are located near the bottom floor of the scene, and one is situated on the sidewall.

 A REAL TUFFY **New Fantasyland, Under the Sea— Journey of The Little Mermaid:** See if you can spot a set of playful frogs at the conclusion of the attraction and an image of everyone's favorite pal!

The frogs are atop lily pads to the left of Ariel and Eric, who are sitting in a boat.

Peter Pan's Flight: Look for your next Hidden Mickey conveniently on the top of the sign for this attraction.

The clouds under Peter's feet form a classic Hidden Mickey.

Peter Pan's Flight: Once inside, and just prior to your journey through Never Land, look for the children's nursery.

On the right side, there is a table with three strategically placed cookies forming the classic Hidden Mickey.

Peter Pan's Flight: Also, just as you begin your flight over the streets of London, look down at the cars on the street for the red one.

This is a very familiar jalopy that looks like Mickey's famous car, which is featured in Mickey's Toontown at Disneyland Park.

Pinocchio Village Haus: This restaurant has been serving Guests since the Magic Kingdom opened its doors in 1971. Scattered throughout the dining location are several murals inspired by the 1940 animated feature it honors. And one mural on the far right back end of the restaurant has two Hidden Mickeys.

One is a small white Hidden Mickey above the letter "s" in the word DREAMS. The other small white Hidden Mickey is situated below the Blue Fairy's hand.

A REAL TUFFY **Princess Fairytale Hall:** If princesses are your thing, then this place, where you can meet and greet some of Disney's legendary princesses, is just for you. As you enter the Royal Gallery prior to meeting your princess, look at the exquisite red curtains in the waiting area.

There you will discover a royal-looking Hidden Mickey fashioned into the curtain fabric.

Rapunzel's Tower: A recent addition to Fantasyland, this beautiful tower is perhaps the prettiest themed restroom in all of the land. On the outside wall of the Rapunzel's Tower area is a collection of pictures of those lively and entertaining tavern patrons from the animated feature *Tangled*.

The picture of the mime is on the outside wall of the ladies' room. His lips, when pressed together, make for a perfect Hidden Mickey.

Sir Mickey's: Inspired by the classic 1938 short *Brave Little Tailor*, this shop features everyone's favorite pal in one of the display windows. In the window that highlights Mickey's attempt at giant hunting, one will find a collection of buttons on the window's floor.

There are two sets of buttons that are strategically placed together to form a Hidden Mickey head.

TOMORROWLAND

Walt Disney was always fascinated by the concept and the excitement of what the future would bring to mankind. Through his many efforts, especially with his television shows—notably the *Man in Space* series—Walt helped introduce to the American public, and to the world, the idea that the future really is a "great big beautiful tomorrow." Today, Tomorrowland resembles more of a galactic spaceport, one envisioned by those early writers and illustrators that dominated our thinking and imagination at the turn of the twentieth century. It is a fictitious place where humans, aliens, and robots coexist and live together in peace.

👉 **Buzz Lightyear's Space Ranger Spin:** Inside the queue, there is a poster on the far right wall as you enter, which reads, **PLANETS OF THE GALLACTIC ALLIANCE**. Study it to discover three Hidden Mickeys.

The first, featured in the Danger Zone known as Sector 9, is on the evil Planet Z. There is a classic Hidden Mickey comprised of craters on the planet's surface.

The second, located in the Gamma Quadrant of Sector 2, is on the green planet Arhyoo, which resembles a bunch of peas clustered together; three of the "peas" form a classic Hidden Mickey.

The third, located on the planet Pollost Prime in Sector 1, is a landmass that's a perfectly shaped side profile of Mickey's head.

Find more versions of these images farther along in the queue, just prior to the scene showing Buzz Lightyear explaining your mission on Space Ranger Spin.

A REAL TUFFY **Buzz Lightyear's Space Ranger Spin:** Once you board a vehicle and are in the first show scene, just when your blasters activate, look quickly down at the far sidewall.

There is a fantastic Hidden Mickey comprised of two smaller blue circles and a green circle for his head.

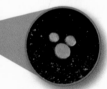

Buzz Lightyear's Space Ranger Spin:
Interestingly, the planet Pollost Prime repeats itself inside as you pass through two other scenes.

The first is in the black chamber room: in this fast-moving scene, the planet Pollost Prime flies by your vehicle, a XP-37 space cruiser. The second is located in one of the final scenes, where your photo is snapped; look to the far left during that moment in your space adventure.

A REAL TUFFY **Buzz Lightyear's Space Ranger Spin:** At the conclusion of the adventure, when you are ready to exit, take a gander at the little green alien mural on the far right wall.

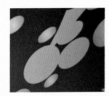

The movie-inspired mural features a Hidden Mickey in the galaxy portion of the mural.

 Buzz Lightyear's Space Ranger Spin: After you step off the ride vehicle, you'll enter a shop that displays the photographs that were taken of you and other Guests during the ride. On the sidewall by the pictures, locate a mural featuring Buzz Lightyear, who's shown surrounded by three green aliens.

Look at the alien in the very front behind the glass. There is a classic Hidden Mickey on his uniform and decal.

 Merchant of Venus: Inside this store, there is a mural on the far left wall with two Hidden Mickeys.

Both feature one of Stitch's cousins and are inspired by the Disney Channel television program Lilo & Stitch, the Series. *One is holding a Mickey head balloon and the other is wearing a set of Mouse ears.*

👍 **Mickey's Star Traders:** A step into this shop is a thrill for any Hidden Mickey seeker! An examination of the mural at the top will reveal six Hidden Mickeys alone.

Look for a Mickey head that forms the futuristic highway, the front facade of a building, the satellite tower of a building, the front of a train, a glass dome on top of a building, and three domes strategically forming a classic Mickey head.

There are also several murals in the shop featuring the lovable mouse in futuristic gear flying a spacecraft.

👉 **Mickey's Star Traders:** Additionally, there are several racks inside the shop with Mickey shapes and images.

At the top of the racks are portholes with various Disney characters in them, including Mickey Mouse.

A REAL TUFFY **Monsters, Inc. Laugh Floor:** Once inside the queue, prior to entering the theater, look to your far right to see a three-panel window featuring futuristic designs of a cityscape.

On the middle panel is a building featuring a dome with a peak. Under the peak of this structure is a cleverly disguised Hidden Mickey.

👍 **Monsters, Inc. Laugh Floor/Buzz Lightyear's Space Ranger Spin:** On the sidewall of Monsters, Inc. Laugh Floor, heading toward Buzz Lightyear's Space Ranger Spin, there are two posters promoting the

Tomorrowland-themed area, where humans, aliens, and robots live together in harmony. Both of these posters feature an array of Hidden Mickeys.

On the poster that reads RECREATIONAL ROCKET VEHICLE SHOW, there is a collection of camping gear in the family's space vehicle featuring a classic Hidden Mickey. There is also a Mickey head directly behind the one child in the spacecraft. And finally, there is a crater in the shape of Mickey on the planet in the poster.

The other poster reads SPACE COLLECTIBLES CONVENTION and has two Mickey shapes. The first is on a pedestal and it is in the shape of a classic Hidden Mickey. The other is located in the food compartment area of the picture. It almost resembles three upside-down cupcakes in the poster.

Space Mountain: Since 1975, Space Mountain has been transporting Guests on an exciting ride through the cosmos; and if you are up for the challenge, you will get to glimpse a Hidden Mickey while inside. However, you have to finish the mission to see it.

As you exit the vehicle and are on the moving sidewalk, take a quick look at the first collection of rocks on your right. A certain three form a classic Hidden Mickey.

Stitch's Great Escape!: Take note of the collection of posters on the far wall soon after entering that focus on the theme of Tomorrowland.

On the one that reads SPACE HOME & GARDEN SHOW, look toward the bottom right corner next to the light fixture; there is a tiny classic turquoise-colored Hidden Mickey.

 Stitch's Great Escape!: Prior to entering the theater and staging area, there is an open window with alien contraptions and gadgetry themed to enhance the experience.

On one panel, there is a set of hieroglyphic-inspired shapes. Tucked among these designs is a classic Hidden Mickey.

👍 **Tomorrowland Transit Authority PeopleMover:** This seven-minute trip will take Guests for a scenic ride throughout Tomorrowland. Buckle up for one scene with a futuristic look at how hair will be done in the future.

On the belt buckle around the waist of the female model, is a classic Hidden Mickey.

👏 **Walt Disney's Carousel of Progress:** Since its debut at the 1964–1965 New York's World Fair, no other theatrical production has been seen by more people who have visited the Disney Parks than Walt Disney's Carousel of Progress. Fittingly, there are six Hidden Mickey images located in the "carousel," all in the final scene when the family in more modern times celebrates Christmas.

The first is a collection of salt and pepper shakers on the kitchen counter featuring a Mickey head that's on the top of each canister.

The second is a plush Mickey Mouse sitting in the midst of Christmas presents under the tree.

There is also a wrapped present underneath the tree and near the grandfather's chair featuring a Mickey head in green on a gift box.

The fourth is a Mickey nutcracker on the mantel of the fireplace.

A REAL TUFFY *The fifth is a wastepaper basket next to the mother who is sitting at a desk with a computer. In the wastepaper basket is a crumpled-up piece of paper and envelope with a Mickey head on the letterhead.*

And finally, in the dining room area behind where the family is situated, there is an abstract painting of Mickey Mouse as the Sorcerer's Apprentice from Fantasia.

👉 **Walt Disney's Carousel of Progress exterior:** At the bottom of the ramp, where the entrance is, there are signs in the shape of cogs.

On the back side of these signs are Hidden Mickey images.

ADVENTURELAND

Adventureland represents the land of the exotic and mysterious. The land was in part inspired by the British Empire of the nineteenth century, a realm that spanned the world—from the jungles of Asia and Africa to the remote locations of the Caribbean and the South Pacific.

👉 **Adventureland entrance:** A short stroll from the hub of Main Street, U.S.A. to Adventureland takes visitors across a bridge to its exotic locales. A set of shields is positioned at the entrance to the bridge.

Two classic Hidden Mickeys are on the shields: one is an upside-down version of everyone's favorite mouse with blue ears at the top of a shield and another, featuring white ears, is at the bottom of a second shield.

Agrabah Bazaar: Adjacent to the marketplace is a jeweled sidewalk representing the mystery of this exotic region.

Situated across from The Magic Carpets of Aladdin is a small charm embedded within the cement sidewalk. This Hidden Mickey is very difficult to spot, given its size and the constant foot traffic in that area.

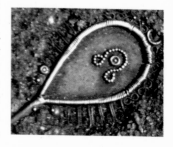

Jungle Cruise: Look directly across the loading dock to discover a Hidden Mickey design on a tree.

A small classic Hidden Mickey in white is on the tree about forty feet off of the ground.

Jungle Cruise: In the African veldt section, there is a legendary scene of a group of explorers climbing a pole as they attempt to avoid the pointed end of a rhinoceros's horn that's thrusting up in the wrong direction, at least from their standpoint.

Slightly to the right, in front of the pole and the rhinoceros, see three rocks that form a classic Hidden Mickey on the ground.

Jungle Cruise: As the boat continues its journey, just prior to entering the hippo bathing pool, look for a crashed plane in the high bushes of the jungle.

On the plane, toward the bottom of it, there are welding screws spread about that form a classic Hidden Mickey on the side of the plane.

Jungle Cruise: See if you can spot a spider with a very familiar mark on its back.

As soon as you enter the Cambodian temple, look to your right; perched in its web is a spider with three spots on the back that form a perfect Hidden Mickey.

👉 **Jungle Cruise:** As you exit the Cambodian temple, look to your left at a column on the left wall.

Located on the third column, marking the end of the temple ruins, is a chipped surface that forms a perfect profile of Minnie's face.

👍 **Pirates of the Caribbean:** In the scene prior to the pirates plundering the town, there is a rather intoxicated pirate who calls himself "Old Bill." He is trying to share his rum with a cat.

The cat casts a shadow of a Hidden Mickey on the wall behind him.

👈 **Pirates of the Caribbean:** In one of the final scenes, there are some unfortunate prisoners who are trying to coax a dog holding the keys to their cell in its mouth.

Take a quick look at the lock on the cellblock door; it resembles a Hidden Mickey.

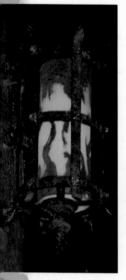

👉 **Pirates of the Caribbean:** There is a collection of lanterns at the end, near the Treasure Room.

The bottoms of the lantern fixtures feature a Mickey head.

A REAL TUFFY **Pirates of the Caribbean:** At the conclusion of the ride, Guests step onto a moving sidewalk and head into an area that has several shops. Once you enter the area, look directly to your left at a painting on the wall.

Find the upper left shoulder of the person in the painting to spot a classic Hidden Mickey.

👍 **Pirates of the Caribbean:** Once you enter the first group of shops, look to your immediate right at a pot of gold coins.

Check the coins carefully. Some of them form a classic Hidden Mickey.

👣 **Swiss Family Treehouse:** The 1960 Disney motion picture *Swiss Family Robinson* provided the inspiration for this place. Find the stone seating areas just outside and look for two Hidden Mickeys that are sure to impress.

First, on the seating area to the left of the attraction's entrance is a classic Hidden Mickey embossed in the stonework.

The second Hidden Mickey, located in the seating across from the Dole Whip Aloha Isle food station, is pressed into the back of the stone bench facing away from the walkway.

A REAL TUFFY **Swiss Family Treehouse:** Hidden Mickey hunters will have to climb the full set of stairs to experience this next Mickey. It is located on the side of the tree amidst a large patch of green algae.

A side profile of Mickey can be spotted as you begin your descent from the top of the tree and head down the trail.

Tortuga Tavern restaurant: There are three candles in a window of this restaurant, across from the Pirates of the Caribbean, which resemble a Hidden Mickey in their alignment.

The window is open and is located toward the back end of the restaurant.

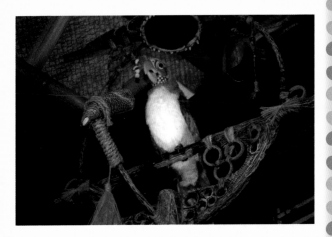

👍 **Walt Disney's Enchanted Tiki Room:** As a result of its popularity at Disneyland, the Enchanted Tiki Room became an opening-day attraction at Walt Disney World's Magic Kingdom. There are two Hidden Mickeys inside, both featured on bird perches.

> *Both birds are similar; the first one is on your left-hand side as you enter the theater in the closest gathering of seats. The second is on the direct opposite side of the theater.*

FRONTIERLAND

Frontierland is the home to cowboys, pioneers, prospectors, big mountain landscapes, and some singing bears. A major draw, billed as the "Wildest Ride in the Wilderness," is Big Thunder Mountain Railroad, which has captivated Guests since its opening in 1980. The small gold-mining town of Tumbleweed serves as the setting for an attraction that resides within a cursed mountain.

 Big Thunder Mountain Railroad: Look down to the right of your moving vehicle to spot a Hidden Mickey as you ascend the hill at the start of the attraction.

Three of the cavern rocks among the stalagmites in the bubbling springs below form a classic Hidden Mickey.

👆 **Frontier Trading Post:** Every great old Western town needs a neighbor mercantile shop, and this one is perfectly themed to Frontierland. Enter the shop through the door on the left to see what loops around.

A lasso on a post forms a classic Hidden Mickey.

👍 **Frontier Trading Post:** At the far right of the shop, on the wall behind the register, is a picture of a cowboy.

A Hidden Mickey is on his lanyard.

👆 **Frontierland Shootin' Arcade:** Take aim at two classic Hidden Mickeys. Both are cacti growing in distinctly Mickey-like shapes.

One is situated in the center of the Frontierland Shootin' Arcade, and the other is on the far right of the attraction.

👉 **Splash Mountain:** The 1946 Disney motion picture *Song of the South* provided the inspiration for this theme park attraction. In the queue directly across from the photo-viewing area, locate a small house that serves as a home for Chip 'n' Dale—and for two Hidden Mickeys.

The first on the small house is made from a collection of acorns above the door.

There is another near the chimney of the house.

👍 **Splash Mountain:** At the beginning of your journey, there is a boiler with the words **MUSKRAT MOONSHINE** painted on the side.

The Hidden Mickey can be found above the "S" in the word MUSKRAT.

👍 **Splash Mountain:** Next, look for a porcupine beating the belly of a turtle like a drum!

On the tree behind him are three pots in the shape of everyone's favorite pal.

Splash Mountain: See if you can spot a picnic basket on a small ledge. It can be seen just past Brer Frog, who is sitting on an alligator and fishing.

Near the basket are three red-and-white-striped fishing bobbers in the shape of a classic Hidden Mickey.

👉 **Splash Mountain:** There is a scene you pass by where Brer Rabbit has been captured by Brer Fox. Look below the two in this scene to discover a Hidden Mickey image.

It is in the shape of a Mickey balloon and is made up of honey.

LIBERTY SQUARE

Liberty Square is a patriotic salute to Colonial times. Featured items include a replica of the Liberty Bell, the Liberty Tree (where many colonists staged their first acts of defiance against British rulers in an effort to be a free nation), and flags representing the thirteen colonies that forged a new nation.

👉 **Columbia Harbour House:** The establishment has a fantastic Hidden Mickey that resides in an old map inside the restaurant.

On the far left wall, there is a themed map featuring three circles that form a classic Hidden Mickey.

👉 **The Hall of Presidents:** Check out a replica of an 1849 portrait of George Washington.

Interestingly—and of course this was not intended—there is a shape that looks like Mickey at the end of Washington's sword.

👉 **Haunted Mansion:** According to the story line, there are 999 happy haunts that occupy the Haunted Mansion, and they are always looking for one more. If you're looking for one more Hidden Mickey, in the ballroom scene, there is a legendary Hidden Mickey on the dining table.

Three plates magically seem to form a classic Hidden Mickey on the ballroom table's left side.

👉 **Haunted Mansion:** There is also a music stand to your right prior to a flight of stairs.

The music stand has a swirl on each side that forms a classic Hidden Mickey.

Haunted Mansion: In the attic, there are two other Hidden Mickeys among the artifacts.

A collection of plates left on the floor

of the attic forms a classic Hidden Mickey, and there's also a hat rack that holds three hats, which as one can observe, strategically form an image of Mickey.

 Haunted Mansion: Finally, there is a ghostly image of a Grim Reaper in the graveyard scene, near the conclusion of the venture.

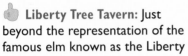

The Grim Reaper is holding an image of a Mickey Mouse head.

 Liberty Tree Tavern: Just beyond the representation of the famous elm known as the Liberty Tree (which served as a gathering place in Boston during the Revolutionary War) is this popular restaurant with two classic Hidden Mickeys. The first is in the waiting area of the restaurant.

Look for a spice rack on a shelf to the right of the fireplace; there are three grapes that form a classic Hidden Mickey in the picture on the rack.

 Liberty Tree Tavern: The other Hidden Mickey is located in the George and Martha Washington Room.

Go up the small flight of stairs and on the side of the far wall above the fireplace is a picture where a Hidden Mickey can be spotted in the clouds.

 Ye Olde Christmas Shoppe: As you cross the bridge from the hub into Liberty Square, this shop is on your left-hand side. Check out the checkout counter.

There is a pile of logs at the bottom of the register area that form a classic Hidden Mickey.

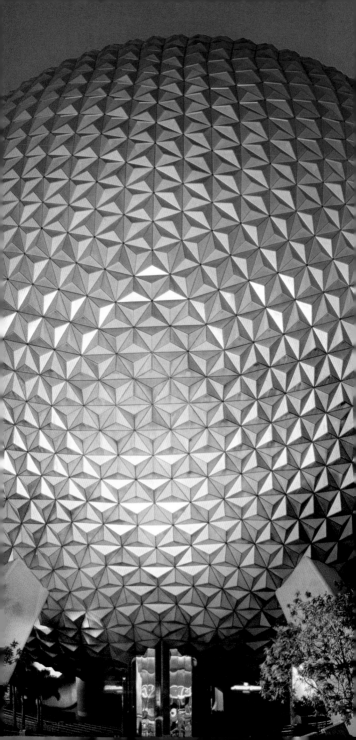

FUTURE WORLD

The Future World experience
is divided into two distinct
sections (Future World East and
Future World West), with an
eighteen-story geodesic sphere
called Spaceship Earth standing
in the middle as one of the most
recognizable structures at any
Disney theme park.

👉 **Club Cool:** Refreshment is the order of the day at this Coca-Cola–inspired outpost. For a cool, familiar shape, locate the banners on the outside of the building.

Heading in the direction of World Showcase, you'll notice the banners feature perfect Hidden Mickeys on them.

👉 **Club Cool:** The establishment allows people to cool off and sample complimentary Coca-Cola soft drinks from around the world. Once inside this taste-testing hub, look for your next salute to the famous mouse on the mural above each soda-dispenser unit.

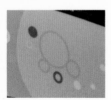

There is a repeating pattern of geometric shapes in this mural. And tucked away in the mural is a perfect collection of circles forming a Hidden Mickey.

👉 **Electric Umbrella:** This fast-food location in the center of Future World serves up its own version of a Hidden Mickey. On the sign advertising the restaurant, there is a very small Hidden Mickey in the purple portion.

The image of Mickey can be seen on the purple pyramid on the top of the sign.

Future World East, Cargo Bay: This shop, which features space-themed gifts, is also home to a payload of Hidden Mickeys. They can be found throughout the store. For example, look up at the beautiful mural on the ceiling.

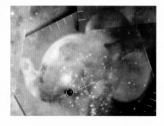

There is a combination of colored gases and stars that form a perfect profile of Mickey on the ceiling in the middle of the shop.

 Future World East, Cargo Bay: There is also a mural on the back wall, behind the cash counter, that is full of Hidden Mickey shapes.

Take a close look at the moon in the mural; there are three craters on it that form a prefect Hidden Mickey.

A REAL TUFFY **Future World East, Cargo Bay:** There is also a traditional Hidden Mickey in the surface of the planet that Mickey and his friends are about to explore.

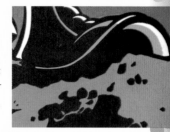

The image of Mickey's head is situated under Minnie's space boot.

 Future World East, Cargo Bay: Notice the reference to the X-2 Deep Space Shuttle in the mural, featured in the Mission: SPACE attraction.

The yellowish vapor stream that is shooting from the back of the X-2 Deep Space Shuttle forms a classic Hidden Mickey.

👉 **Future World East, Cargo Bay:** There are also two faint Hidden Mickeys among the star cluster.

Just below the spacecraft are two faint images of Mickey formed by three celestial bodies.

👉 **Future World East, Cargo Bay:** In addition, there is a collection of Hidden Mickeys on the walls you walk past prior to exiting the establishment.

The images of Mickey come in a variety of shapes and sizes and are featured on the left and right walls around the exit. The Mickey shapes are in the form of electrical covers and boxes that are attached to the walls.

 Future World East, Mission: SPACE: The dark side of the moon remains a deep mystery. So, who is to say there isn't a representation of Mickey found among the craters of the moon?

On the moon located at the entrance to the attraction, there are various Hidden Mickeys. They all appear on the back side of the moon; each one is formed by three craters, which strategically fit together to form a Hidden Mickey.

👉 **Future World East, Mission: SPACE:** As you approach the attraction, look for a series of jeweled patterns on the sidewalk.

Look carefully for two Hidden Mickeys formed by three jewels in the cement.

 Future World East, Mission: SPACE: While on your imaginative journey to Mars, in your X-2 Deep Space Shuttle, observe carefully the landing deck as you approach the planet.

You will discover a set of three devices that resemble some communication devices that form a classic Hidden Mickey.

👉 **Future World East, Test Track:** This high-octane adventure also pays tribute to the famous mouse. There is a film sequence Guests may watch while they are in the queue area, which features a collection of children who speak about the type of automobile they are about to create.

Look closely at the wall to the right of the screen. There is a black shadow of Mickey's head.

👍 **Future World East, Test Track:** Guests can discover their next Hidden Mickey while aboard their test vehicle in the environmental chamber.

Check each side of the third environmental chamber; inside, there is circuitry that forms a classic Hidden Mickey when it is fully lit.

 Future World West, Journey into Imagination with Figment: Dr. Nigel Channing, chairman of the Imagination

Institute, invites Guests to the institute's Open House for a tour through the Sensory Labs, which demonstrates how the five human senses help capture and control the imagination. In the room that focuses on the sense of sight, try to spot the image of Mickey.

If you focus on the whiteboard in the Sight Room, you'll spot a Mickey head that's been drawn on it.

Future World West, Journey into Imagination with Figment: The next set of Hidden Mickey images can all be found in the mischievous purple dragon Figment's Upside Down Room.

Notice Figment in the tub with the large collection of bubbles; three bubbles near his hand form a perfect Hidden Mickey.

Future World West, Journey into Imagination with Figment: Items atop the Upside Down Room's table also serve up their own style of Hidden Mickey.

The onion rings, which are located on the table, are arranged in a way that resembles a traditional Hidden Mickey.

A REAL TUFFY **Future World West, Journey into Imagination with Figment:** And, don't forget to take a quick peek inside Figment's Upside Down Room refrigerator.

Some eggs on one shelf form a classic Hidden Mickey.

Future World West, The Land pavilion:
The pavilion features a beautiful collection of globes and a salute to the four seasons: winter, spring, summer, and fall. There is a center globe, which is an interpretation of the Earth and home to a Hidden Mickey image.

There is a collection of swirls in the water right off the coast of South America that make up a Hidden Mickey.

Future World West, The Land pavilion, The Garden Grill Restaurant: This specialty themed restaurant is known for offering a variety of seasonal tastes and cuisines while the venue slowly rotates to provide Guests a unique circular view of their surroundings. The restaurant also dishes up its own unique version of Mickey. Look closely at the mural on the inside wall.

In the first set of ferns to your right, there is a three-dimensional-looking head of Mickey peering through the trees.

Future World West, The Land pavilion, Living with the Land: As you are about to board your boat and begin your educational journey, take a look at the beautiful mural on the back wall.

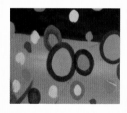

There are a few references to Mickey on the mural formed by three repeating shapes and circles found throughout the painting.

👍 **Future World West, The Land pavilion, Living with the Land:** Guests of all ages gain a newfound appreciation for where their food comes from on this cruise through the living laboratories inside this pavilion. And inside this garden oasis is a collection of references to Mickey in living form.

There are several examples inside this attraction of fruits, vegetables, and plants that are groomed and designed to resemble Mickey.

👍 **Future World West, The Land pavilion, Living with the Land:** Aquaculture is known as the farming of aquatic organisms, such as fish, crustaceans, mollusks, and aquatic plants. This practice takes center stage inside the attraction. In fact, there is a set of fish tanks growing a collection of aquatic life.

Take notice of the one tank which features a reference to both Minnie and Mickey in hidden form.

👍 **Future World West, The Land pavilion, Living with the Land:** In that same general area, look for a hose on the platform floor.

The hose on the platform has been strategically and logically shaped to represent a perfect Hidden Mickey.

Future World West, The Land pavilion, Living with the Land: See if you can spot the microplates that are in the window of one of the viewing areas of the research and education center for the attraction.

There is a set of microplates in the window that features a substance in certain holes that depict a perfect Hidden Mickey.

Future World West, The Land pavilion, Soarin': Before you fly away on your journey over California, you will have to spend a few brief moments with your chief flight attendant, Patrick, who will give you some much-needed safety messages. There are also two fun, if not-so-hidden, Mickeys incorporated into the safety message and film.

At one point during the film sequence, our chief flight attendant, Patrick, asks a Guest to remove his set of Mouse ears before the flight can proceed.

There is also an image of a child being helped with his safety harness. The child is wearing a pair of pants with Mickey Mouse on them; and interestingly, the shirt features Grumpy.

Future World West, The Land pavilion, Soarin': There are also several Hidden Mickey images that can be found in the standby queue line for the attraction.

They are featured in the game sequences as you move along the queue line.

Future World West, The Land pavilion, Soarin': During the presentation of the attraction, a series of

three Hidden Mickeys can be seen as you approach a
golf course in Palm Springs, California.

 *There are three trees in the foreground that form a
shadow in the shape of the famous mouse.*

*There is also an individual holding a Mickey balloon
next to the golfing party that is about to tee off.*

 *There is also a golfer who's hitting a golf ball off of a
tee. Pay attention as the ball approaches the screen:
take notice of the Mickey head that is on the front of the
ball.*

👍 **Future World West, The Land pavilion, Soarin':**
What day would be complete at Disneyland without
that symbolic Disney kiss good night and a fireworks
display—and Mickey?

*There are three fireworks that burst and
form a perfect Hidden Mickey.*

✋ **Future World West, The Seas with Nemo &
Friends pavilion:** Before you throw out that piece of
trash, while at the pavilion, check out the receptacle
for your next Hidden Mickey.

Tucked away on the side of this beautifully themed trash can is the logo for the Nemo attraction and a collection of bubbles that form a traditional Hidden Mickey design.

👉 **Future World West, The Seas with Nemo & Friends pavilion:** Inspired by the 2003 Disney • Pixar film *Finding Nemo*, this attraction takes Guests on a whimsical journey under the "Big Blue World" while riding in a "clamobile." The saltwater aquarium provides a perfectly themed backdrop during your journey, but it's the carefully sculpted rockwork of the attraction that showcases three Hidden Mickeys.

Look for a debossed image of Mickey when passing the first collection of coral.

The ride vehicle passes under a rock formation which features a Hidden Mickey on its underside.

The third Hidden Mickey may be viewed when you see Dory for the first time and she is helping to look for "Fabio." Again, there is an indentation on the rock that forms a traditional Hidden Mickey.

🚲 **Future World West, The Seas with Nemo & Friends pavilion:** Before your journey comes to an end, enjoy a ride along the East Australian Current (EAC) and hang ten with Crush the sea turtle and his friends. You can also catch a quick glimpse of another Hidden Mickey.

This Mickey is formed by a collection of bubbles coming together along the EAC.

🐟 **Future World West, The Seas with Nemo & Friends pavilion:** Marine biologists have undertaken to replace the beloved starfish's name with the term sea star because, well, the starfish is not a fish! It's an echinoderm, closely related to sea urchins and sand dollars. The sea star also has no brain! Yet, Peach, the beloved starfish, or rather the beloved sea star, from *Finding Nemo*, has a plethora of knowledge and facts she is willing to recite. For example, as you conclude your journey, Peach can recite to you how many Guests experienced the attraction the day before.

Three of Peach's suckers form a perfect Hidden Mickey.

🐟 **Future World West, The Seas with Nemo & Friends pavilion, aquarium:** Besides hosting some unique attractions, the pavilion has also provided marine support, research, and a place for observation over the years for some of the ocean's most cherished inhabitants. (One such effort focuses on the protection and study of the manatee population.) To that end, if you examine the blackboard showcasing two of the pavilion's most recent residents, you can spot your next Hidden Mickey.

Look at the statistics associated with the two manatees and you will discover a Hidden Mickey head on the blackboard.

👍 **Future World West, The Seas with Nemo & Friends pavilion, aquarium:** The 5.7- million-gallon saltwater aquarium is also the recipient of a very unique Hidden Mickey offering.

In the back tank area, there are strategically placed rocks on the bottom surface of the aquarium that were arranged by some skilled Disney divers in the shape of Mickey's head.

🐟 **Future World West, The Seas with Nemo & Friends pavilion, Coral Reef Restaurant:** This themed restaurant serves up a variety of seasonal and traditional seafood favorites while a view of the aquarium provides a picturesque backdrop to your dining experience. The restaurant also serves up a variety of Hidden Mickey shapes and designs. For example, located between the first and second landing in the middle of the restaurant is a staircase featuring

a marble-themed pillar.

On the front face of this blue pillar are three tiles perfectly shaped to resemble Mickey.

A REAL TUFFY **Future World West, The Seas with Nemo & Friends pavilion, Coral Reef Restaurant:** There are also two other Hidden Mickey shapes in the beautifully themed tile work. Both are located behind the Guests' seating areas, and both are in the middle of the restaurant.

One is on the first landing, and the other is on the second. They are both featured in a variety of colors.

👉 **Future World West, The Seas with Nemo & Friends pavilion, Turtle Talk with Crush:** Another favorite from *Finding Nemo* is Crush, the more than one-hundred-year-old sea turtle. Crush hosts his very own interactive attraction and comes to life on the sea screen to communicate with

those audience members wanting to know more about his unique life! If you want to know more about a Hidden Mickey or two, don't go too far in.

The sign as you enter the attraction features three bubbles just under the jaw of Crush that resemble a perfect Hidden Mickey.

👎 **Future World West, The Seas with Nemo & Friends pavilion, Turtle Talk with Crush:** You don't have to travel the length of the EAC to discover your next Hidden Mickey. Just around the right corner from the attraction's entrance is a picture featuring aquatic shapes.

On this panel, notice a small black Hidden Mickey created by an arrangement of various aquatic shapes.

👎 **Mouse Gear:** As the name suggests, this shop is a perfect salute to Mickey and your one-stop location for all Mickey souvenir needs. The store is also bursting with a vast collection of Hidden Mickey images in every shape and size.

Look for the gears, wing nuts, and cogs that are scattered throughout the shop; each one forms a classic Hidden Mickey image.

In addition, there are a variety of boiler hatches and temperature gauges that form a Mickey head.

Take a close look at the merchandise racks and displays for additional Hidden Mickey shapes.

A REAL TUFFY **Spaceship Earth:** One of the first Hidden Mickey images is featured in a mural that's on display right as you are about to enter the attraction from the queue area. The mural details man's history with communications. Look for the communications satellite in the mural, and concentrate on the markings on the spacecraft with the number 2350.

Notice the "3," which is in black, unlike the other digits. The inside of the 3 also resembles a set of Mouse ears.

 Spaceship Earth: In one scene, a gathering of Middle Eastern and Turkish scholars is shown; it highlights the libraries they created and the data collection they provided for future generations. Now, look across from those scholars who are on the left of the moving vehicle and you'll see that there is a bookshelf with ancient scrolls.

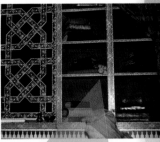

The last set of scrolls form a classic Hidden Mickey.

A REAL TUFFY **Spaceship Earth:** Guests soon arrive at a monastery, where biblical manuscripts are being painstakingly copied by ancient monks. One monk—who has fallen asleep—is working on a manuscript that bears a mouse-shaped mark.

Toward the tip of his writing instrument is a black mark that resembles a traditional Hidden Mickey.

 Spaceship Earth: Your time machine vehicle soon takes you to the dawn of the Renaissance, where art and culture dominated many regions of the world for more than three hundred years. Look at the artist's table as soon as you enter this show scene.

The artist's table on your left features three circles, formed from dried paint residue; the white circles left behind make a perfect Hidden Mickey.

A REAL TUFFY Spaceship Earth: The Renaissance period you're traveling through is also home to your next Hidden Mickey. Concentrate on the still life painting of fruit, cheese, and wine.

Look carefully at the bowl containing the fruit; the large orange and two smaller pieces of fruit make for a perfect Hidden Mickey.

👉 **Spaceship Earth:** The next scene takes Guests through a romanticized view of the twentieth century and the dawn of the communications revolution. Here you can discover a collection of hidden gems scattered throughout the show scene—one of which salutes the Mouse.

Look for the sign advertising the first color animated short starring Mickey Mouse: The Band Concert (1935).

A REAL TUFFY **Spaceship Earth:** Look very carefully at the ticket booth and the woman who is holding a newspaper in this show scene. The paper shows the main headline reflecting the Gold Medal victories of Jesse Owens during the 1936 Summer Olympic Games in Berlin, Germany.

Above that listing on the newspaper is a hidden reference to Mickey: MICKEY MOUSE COMIC INSIDE.

👍 **Spaceship Earth:** There is also a subtle little salute to Mickey in the show scene that features the family watching television as the Apollo 11 astronauts are about to take their first steps on the moon.

There is a component from the board game Mouse

Trap lost behind the sofa where the family is sitting and watching the lunar landing. Mouse Trap was a popular game developed by Ideal (now Hasbro) and first introduced in 1963.

WORLD SHOWCASE

The richness and diversity of the human experience is on display at World Showcase. Since this original Epcot mainstay opened with the Park in 1982, World Showcase has been a "community of nations." World Showcase has always been a living laboratory with a purpose to accentuate and highlight the many cultures, traditions, and accomplishments of people from around the world. This is the essence of World Showcase: representing a collective endeavor by a people and their hope for a better tomorrow.

☞ **American Adventure pavilion,** *Building a Future Together* **(painting):** This painting details the entrepreneurial spirit that helped fuel the massive expansion of our cities, like New York, and led to breakthroughs in construction and the dawn of the skyscraper and the era of modernized building. Look

carefully at the open beam to the left and right sides of the construction workers in the painting.

There are holes where rivets will eventually go that form a traditional-looking Hidden Mickey.

☞ **American Adventure pavilion,** *Defending Freedom* **(painting):** Concentrate on the nose of the plane for an image of Mickey.

Tucked strategically in the nose of the plane is a faint black-shadowed Hidden Mickey.

 American Adventure pavilion, *Election Day* **(painting):** Look for a bunch of roses during your hunt for the next Hidden Mickey.

Situated in the bottom portion of the painting is a woman who wears a hat decorated with roses. The roses form a classic Hidden Mickey.

☞ **American Adventure pavilion,** *Reaching for the Stars* **(painting):** This painting celebrates the advancement of spaceflight with an image of one of the space shuttles and its early missions. Concentrate on the blueprints in the picture on the far right side.

The tail and body of the shuttle resembles a classic Hidden Mickey.

 American Adventure pavilion, *Seeds of Hope* (painting): This portrait explores the friendship forged between our early settlers and Native Americans, who taught those pioneers the fine art of farming as a means of survival. *Seed* anything else?

A closer look at a collection of seeds the person is planting in the foreground of the picture reveals a traditional Hidden Mickey.

A REAL TUFFY **American Adventure pavilion, *Westward Ho!* (painting):** This painting offers some insight into the westward expansion of the United States and the struggles that followed. Look at the oxen in the middle of the painting.

On the side of one particular ox, there is a faint black Hidden Mickey between the front and hind legs.

American Adventure pavilion, rotunda: Look for the large bronze doors that dominate the rotunda for your next set of Hidden Mickeys. They can be found on the far left and right rear walls, both on the first and second floors.

These large bronze doors feature repeating classic Hidden Mickey designs in each corner.

👆 **American Adventure pavilion, rotunda:** Don't go too far for your next Hidden Mickey because it is also on the bronze doors in the rotunda area! There is a majestic image of an eagle located on each door.

To the left of the proud bird, there is a flower with petals and two additional elements— combining to resemble a traditional Hidden Mickey.

👆 **Canada pavilion, Le Cellier Steakhouse:** You won't be disappointed if you decide to take your Hidden Mickey hunt inside this signature restaurant. Directly behind the check-in desk, spot a wine cabinet featuring a vast selection of wines.

Three bottles on the top rack are strategically positioned to form a classic Hidden Mickey.

A REAL TUFFY **Canada pavilion, Northwest Mercantile:** Reminiscent of the traditional trading posts that were spread throughout the vast Canadian Northwest, this shop calls on all Hidden Mickey hunters to go "fishing." As soon as you enter the front entrance, look up at a box on a high shelf.

A fish hangs on the outside of the crate. On the side of the fish, three spots form a traditional Hidden Mickey.

👆 **Canada pavilion, on the grounds:** The Native Americans of the Pacific Northwest coast carved magnificent vertical cedar columns, known as totem poles. As a salute to this ancient art, the Raven stands proudly as a centerpiece of the Canada pavilion. It is also home to two classic Hidden Mickey shapes.

Look carefully at the top of the Raven totem poles on both sides of the structure. Near the wings of the legendary creature is a classic Hidden Mickey.

Canada pavilion, on the grounds: There is a refreshment cart at the pavilion's entrance, along the promenade. Look directly across from the cart to a fence.

This Hidden Mickey is carved into the top fence rail.

China pavilion, Temple of Heaven: Sitting as the pavilion's cornerstone is this impressive temple, which was inspired by the original fourteenth-century structure located in the heart of Beijing; it is also home to one classic Hidden Mickey. Perhaps this image was purely by accident, but nonetheless there

are three circles that form a famous shape.

Under each circular eave of the building, there is a repeating upside-down Hidden Mickey motif.

France pavilion, Les Vins de France: Known for having some of the finest vineyards in all the world, France truly rules when it comes to wine. The offerings at this classic Paris-inspired shop are apt to please the palate of any connoisseur.

Prior to stepping into this establishment, look up at the columns on either side of the entrance. There are Mickey-inspired shapes molded into the columns.

👈 **France pavilion, Monsieur Paul:** Guests will not only indulge in classic French cuisine at this restaurant, but may also notice that it's home to a couple of traditional Hidden Mickeys.

Look for swirly-shaped Mickey heads on the marquee at the restaurant's entrance, as well as on the top of the menu display.

👆 **France pavilion, on the grounds:** Inspired by the Paris landmark known as Les Halles—a marketplace featuring shops and restaurants—this area in the France pavilion is home to two classic Hidden Mickeys. Look down at the bases of the trees scattered in the marketplace.

The metal grates surrounding the bases of the trees feature a repeating Hidden Mickey design.

👆 **France pavilion, on the grounds:** There is also a garden area featuring a collection of beautifully groomed small bushes. Look toward the middle of these bushes.

You should discover a small bush that has been perfectly cut and fashioned to resemble Mickey's head.

Germany pavilion, Das Kaufhaus: Loosely translated the word *kaufhaus* means, "The place to buy or purchase." It may also be the perfect place to discover your next Hidden Mickey.

On the courtyard side of the pavilion, look closely at the sculpture of the first German king mounted on the second floor of the shop's exterior.

The king's crown features a perfect Hidden Mickey.

 Germany pavilion, Das Kaufhaus: See if you can spot the picture of "Das Mouse" in traditional German garb.

The picture of Mickey Mouse is featured on a wall behind the checkout counter to the left of the traditional cuckoo clocks that hang from the store's wall. Mickey is wearing traditional lederhosen and German clothing.

 Germany pavilion, Karamell-Küche: If you can tear your eyes away from the delectable caramel creations in the display window outside this sweetshop, see if you can spot a cookbook.

In the picture of caramel apples featured in the cookbook, the forward-most apple sports three spots of reflected light that converge to make a Hidden Mickey.

👉 **Germany pavilion, Karamell-Küche:** Two more Mickey designs are cleverly masked inside this confectionery workshop and store. Find the mural from the shop's sponsor that reads, **THE WERTHER'S ORIGINAL STORY**.

> *Look very carefully on the mural, just below the words THE WERTHER'S ORIGINAL STORY; there is a faint Hidden Mickey on the side of the mountain.*

A REAL TUFFY **Germany pavilion, Karamell-Küche:** Next head toward the back of this artisan's delight to the shop door closest to the World Showcase promenade. Nearby, inside the shop, a small Mickey head is painted on the side panel of a shelf display.

> *The small orange classic Hidden Mickey is part of the vine motif on the side panel of the shelf display nearest to the door.*

👆 **Italy pavilion, Enoteca Castello:** During the mile-and-a-half journey around the World Showcase promenade, Guests are certainly treated to a unique mix of food and drink specialties that epitomize each country and/or region. This shop, which is known for some dazzling wine choices, is no exception. Can you find a Hidden Mickey in the wood?

> *Inside the wine shop, a classic Hidden Mickey is featured in the woodwork relief design on the front of the wine counter.*

 Italy pavilion, Enoteca Castello: Three generations of Italy's Mariani family have built Banfi Vintners into one of America's finest names in imported wines. Their shop also features another Hidden Mickey design, but this one's at the bottom of a wine rack.

> *The wine rack is located along the side of the shop, near the wine counter. The grillwork of the wine rack forms a swirly interpretation of Mickey.*

A REAL TUFFY **Italy pavilion, Neptune Fountain:** Inspired by the original version located in the Piazza della Signoria, in Florence, Italy, the fountain takes center stage in the pavilion's courtyard. While you're admiring the god of the sea, look out for a traditional Hidden Mickey.

> *On the back left wall of the fountain behind Neptune, look for a depression in the rock that forms a perfect Hidden Mickey.*

 Japan pavilion, on the grounds: Tranquility is certainly the inspiration for this Japanese-inspired koi pond at the entrance to the pavilion. Huge, beautiful fish dominate the pond area, along with one Hidden Mickey.

> *Look for the drain hole in the pond with a metal grate covering the opening. A quick peek will reveal a classic, submerged Hidden Mickey.*

👍 **Japan pavilion, on the grounds:** There are also numerous Japanese-inspired trees scattered throughout the site outside the pavilion. Look down at the roots of the trees.

The metal grates surrounding the bases of the trees feature a repeating Hidden Mickey design.

A REAL TUFFY **Mexico pavilion, Gran Fiesta Tour Starring the Three Caballeros:** This attraction takes Guests on a whimsical journey through the history of Mexico—with three familiar and famous fowl: Donald Duck, Panchito, and José Carioca! The attraction also hosts a wide assortment of Hidden Mickeys. At the first turn on your boat ride, check out the art depicting pre-Columbian civilizations.

Look at the native in the middle of the wall art and study his necklace. The bright blue circles comprising the center of the necklace resemble a traditional Hidden Mickey.

A REAL TUFFY **Mexico pavilion, Gran Fiesta Tour Starring the Three Caballeros:** In the same painting, look for the individual who is wearing the alligator-inspired headpiece.

Notice the staff being held by the man behind him. Near the top there is a disk with three circles that form a Hidden Mickey.

👈 **Mexico pavilion, Gran Fiesta Tour Starring the Three Caballeros:** This attraction was originally called El Río del Tiempo, "The River of Time," and, now, it is time for another Hidden Mickey clue! Look for the traditional image of Mickey's head when a small baby octopus introduces herself to Donald while he is taking a quick dip.

*A Hidden Mickey is formed in the small
lagoon by a combination of moving bubbles.*

👉 **Mexico pavilion, Gran Fiesta Tour Starring the
Three Caballeros:** Next, on the left side of your boat,
examine a small barge with the words VIVA DONALD.
The barge is filled with a collection of trinkets and
souvenirs that apparently
Donald has collected
while on his journey.

*See if you can spot
the three drums on
the bottom right
corner of the barge
that form a perfect
Hidden Mickey.*

👍 **Mexico pavilion, Gran Fiesta Tour Starring the
Three Caballeros:** As your journey through Mexico
comes to its conclusion, look at the fiber-optic effects
that create fireworks along the ceiling.

*Take a quick gander. You may see an assortment
of fireworks that form a classic Hidden Mickey.*

👉 **Mexico pavilion, Gran Fiesta Tour Starring the
Three Caballeros:** As you exit the attraction, look for
your next Hidden Mickey when you pass between the
handrails that lead from the unload area and funnel
Guests into the main concourse.

*Look at the wooden beam
to your left. Etched in the
inside wooden beam of the
handrail is a distorted
Mickey shape.*

👉 **Mexico pavilion, interior pyramid:** This Hidden Mickey can best be spotted from either the back portion of the San Angel Inn Restaurante or from the Gran Fiesta Tour Starring the Three Caballeros attraction. Look up at the themed pyramid and then shift your focus to the right of the smoking volcano.

There is a faint Hidden Mickey just above the tree line of the lush jungle forest.

👉 **Mexico pavilion, San Angel Inn Restaurante:** The restaurant overlooks an indoor lagoon with a backdrop featuring a pyramid and a smoking volcano; it also features a fun little Hidden Mickey in the very back right portion of the restaurant, heading toward a small gate near the lagoon.

Take a quick look over the gate to find a Hidden Mickey in the depression of the rock in the middle of the second step from the landing.

👉 **Morocco pavilion, The Brass Bazaar:** Henna lamps, wooden boxes, brass plates and bowls, and other antiquities of this proud and ancient land are on display in this shop. On display, too, is a classic Hidden Mickey design; it's toward the back of the shop.

On the sidewall, take note of a set of three brass plates positioned to resemble everyone's favorite mouse.

A REAL TUFFY **Morocco pavilion, character meet and greet:** No visit to Morocco would be complete without capturing a photo with everyone's favorite "street rat" and the princess whose heart he stole. The character meet-and-greet area featuring Aladdin and Jasmine has a perfect Agrabah-inspired backdrop—which contains three salutes to Mickey.

The first Hidden Mickey is located in a tower on the mural's right side; the second is in a dark archway on the left side of the picture; and the third is in the main street toward the middle.

👉 **Morocco pavilion, Outdoor Bazaar:** Just outside The Brass Bazaar is an outdoor market filled with an array of handmade crafts, and a nod to Mickey. Look up on the top wall of the outdoor market and you

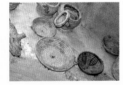

will see a collection of baskets hanging on the wall.

Find the three in particular that form a perfect Hidden Mickey.

👍 **Morocco pavilion, Souk-Al-Magreb ("Gifts of Morocco"):** Located on the pavilion's waterside walkway, this shop stocks authentic Moroccan clothing, crafts, and trinkets. It is also the home to a classic Hidden Mickey.

Hanging on the open door to the shop are three plates—two small ones and one large—forming a perfect Hidden Mickey.

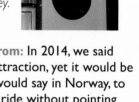

👆 **Morocco pavilion, Tangierine Café:** Serving up Mediterranean staples such as hummus, tabouleh, and falafel, this eatery is found inside the Koutoubia Minaret. It also serves up two Hidden Mickey designs on its outside wall.

Look above the side entrance at mosaic tiles that form the traditional Mickey shape.

👆 **Morocco pavilion, Tangierine Café:** Once inside, observe the far left wall near the specialty drink and refreshment section and find a few plates featuring the restaurant logo.

Together, the three plates hung on the wall form a perfect Hidden Mickey.

👆 **Norway pavilion, Maelstrom:** In 2014, we said good-bye to the Maelstrom attraction, yet it would be difficult to bid *farvel*, as they would say in Norway, to this fondly remembered boat ride without pointing out one quintessential Hidden Mickey that used to exist on the large mural behind the loading area.

The painting detailed the history of Norway, beginning with the Vikings to present-day life. On the far-left portion of the wall, there was a Norseman seated in a Viking longship who was wearing a set of Mouse ears.

Outpost: This refreshment oasis is also the site of two Hidden Mickey shapes. Look for one of the middle huts with a thatched roof along the World Showcase promenade and find a set of luggage near the rooftop.

One piece of luggage includes a name tag with the words M. MOUSE; and just to the right of the luggage tag, there is a VOYAGE sticker with the name MICKEY MOUSE spelled out.

👆 **United Kingdom pavilion, Rose & Crown Pub & Dining Room:** True to the name of this pub and restaurant, the design on the front doors of this fine establishment features a rose, a crown, and other flourishes—arranged in a familiar shape.

The etched-glass design in the center circular wood frame evokes the image of Mickey's head, with a crown atop it.

👆 **United Kingdom pavilion, Sportsman's Shoppe:** Designed to resemble a traditional Tudor castle, this shop is dedicated to the countries that make up the United Kingdom and their appreciation for all sports. A sign out front contains several sports-related icons that should be examined.

Together, a tennis racquet, a rugby ball, and a soccer ball form a traditional Hidden Mickey shape.

DISNEY'S
HOLLYWOOD
STUDIOS

HOLLYWOOD BOULEVARD

Marking the Park's entrance is the Crossroads of the World structure featuring Mickey Mouse, as a cleverly disguised lightning rod. The icon was inspired by the original structure (with that same name) located at the intersection of Sunset Boulevard and Las Palmas in Los Angeles—and often considered America's first out-door shopping mall.

👉 **Adrian & Edith's Head to Toe:** From Mouse ears to apparel, this costume designer–inspired store is the place to buy embroidered clothing. Look carefully up on the top shelf of the store.

Can you spot a large Asian-inspired fan with a Hidden Mickey among its fan slats?

👍 **Backlot Express:** There are several Mickey images on the bulletin boards hanging in the restaurant. All of the references to Mickey seem to reside in the portion of the restaurant closest to Star Tours—The Adventures Continue.

One Mickey image can be found on the far back wall of the restaurant in a small alcove. The other is located on the wall adjacent to the Star Tours attraction near the side door.

There is also an image of Mickey on a paint can above the restaurant's beverage dispenser.

👟 **Celebrity 5 & 10:** This establishment is inspired by a real-life version of a famous store, J. J. Newberry, which stood as a centerpiece on Hollywood Boulevard for many years beginning in 1928. Here, at the Park's version of the store, study the window displays for a secret.

You will see a collection of swirly shapes—with classic Hidden Mickeys among them—in the corner of those displays.

👉 **Cover Story:** At this place, which serves your PhotoPass needs, study the outside structure for several Hidden Mickey shapes.

Just below the second floor windows, there are Mouse ears in the exterior design of the building.

👆 **Cover Story:** Inside the shop, there is a picture of Walt Disney and some of his animation team on the back wall. Spot anything else?

There is a gold Mickey head on the top of the picture.

A REAL TUFFY **Cover Story:** Outside of the shop, locate a picture promoting a fictitious movie called *It Crawled from Darkness*.

The Hidden Mickey nests within the words MOUSE HOUSE PICTURES in the left-hand corner of the poster.

✌️ **The Darkroom:** This shop focuses on camera-related goods. Look closely at the store's window display.

You'll spot a series of Mickey-themed trophies scattered throughout the window display. There is also a small replica sign advertising WALT DISNEY'S SILLY SYMPHONY cartoon series proudly featuring Mickey Mouse.

A REAL TUFFY **Echo Lake, 50's Prime Time Café:** Mom is in the kitchen, and Sis or Cousin might take your order in this perfectly themed restaurant that embellishes how life was during the 1950s. References to Mickey can be found while you watch your "Disney" brand television at your table.

One of the television shows you are treated to during your dining experience is the Mickey Mouse Club. *Other programming includes the Opening Day ceremony special for Disneyland (which aired on July 17, 1955), and a commercial that features windup Mickey and his friends.*

A REAL TUFFY **Echo Lake, Hollywood & Vine:** Here's a family-style eatery that pays tribute to a famous Hollywood intersection and also has two classic Hidden Mickeys found inside. Look for the mural map of the San Fernando Valley on the far left wall of the restaurant.

On the far right side of this mural is a stick figure of Mickey Mouse.

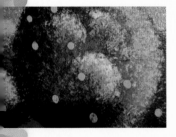

Once you find this first Hidden Mickey, look slightly to the left; there is a line of trees. Among those, there is one which definitely forms the shape of Mickey's head.

👆 **Echo Lake, Peevy's Frozen Concoctions:** A small place inspired by the 1991 Disney motion picture *The Rocketeer*, Peevy's is also home to a Hidden Mickey. You'll find it situated on the side street between Hollywood Boulevard and Echo Lake, near Keystone Clothiers.

Once there, look for a set of welding tanks whose gauges seem to resemble Mickey.

👆 **Echo Lake, Tune-In Lounge:** This is the themed waiting and lounge area adjacent to the 50's Prime Time Café. Notice the tabletops in the lounge area.

See if you can spot the Hidden Mickey shapes that are forged into the tops of some of the tables.

👆 **The Great Movie Ride:** In the great tradition of placing celebrity handprints in the cement outside the original Grauman's Chinese Theatre (which began happening in 1927), the practice was repeated for many years at the Park's version (but with hand and footprints). During the "Footprint Ceremony" for Harry Anderson's and Carol Burnett's separate squares, the two added their own version of a Hidden Mickey.

Anderson added three dots to his tie in the cement, forming a classic Hidden Mickey.
Burnett painted a caricature of herself wearing Mouse ears.

A REAL TUFFY **The Great Movie Ride:** A fantastic Hidden Mickey hides in the loading dock area of this attraction, which is an ultimate salute to some of Hollywood's greatest movies of all time.

> *In the mural on the left side of the ride vehicle, look at the third to the last house on the hill at the end of the mural. There is a silhouette of Mickey Mouse at one of the windows on the top floor of the house.*

The Great Movie Ride: The loading dock features a salute to Minnie Mouse in the same mural. She is featured in side-profile form.

> *Find the house that features just the peak of the hacienda. The house is situated near the middle of the mural. Minnie is positioned just above the house's peak, and she is distinguishable by the bow in her hair.*

The Great Movie Ride: In the gangster shoot-out scene, there is a poster for the motion picture *The Public Enemy* starring the great James Cagney. Once you spot the poster, look at the bottom near the Colgate advertisement.

The poster and advertisement appear to have been placed over another poster that features Mickey Mouse; you can see a bit of his leg and shoe.

 **The Great Movie Ride:** In the same gangster shoot-out scene, look up to your left (way up, in fact) toward the top window.

There in the upper window you will discover a silhouette of Mickey Mouse in one of the window panels.

 **The Great Movie Ride:** The next scene along your journey is referred to as the bandit scene. Look for a crate filled with horseshoes on the left side of your ride vehicle. Three horseshoes are placed strategically together to form a classic Hidden Mickey.

The crate is on the floor of the attraction, on the bandit's side, near the exit of the show scene.

 **The Great Movie Ride:** The "Well of Souls" scene, a tribute to archaeologist professor Indiana Jones and the Lost Ark, is also home to several hidden gems. On the right side of your ride vehicle, for example, are two Hidden Mickeys.

 On the far wall of the scene is a collection of hieroglyphic images, and tucked away in the various symbols is a Hidden Mickey.

The next Hidden Mickey is found on the floor of the Well of Souls, in front of Indy and Sallah, as they lift the ark. The Mickey head can clearly be found on the facing of an ancient tablet.

The Great Movie Ride: Your next Hidden Mickey in the "Well of Souls" scene can be found on the left side of your ride vehicle with a Mickey and Donald in hieroglyphic form.

The two images are on the far side of the wall and to the right of the second large statue.

 The Great Movie Ride: In the Tarzan scene, there is a tree with a bird's nest in its branches. Three tiny eggs form a classic Hidden Mickey.

The tree is located on the right side of the ride vehicle where Tarzan, as played by actor Johnny Weissmuller, begins his classic swing from the branches.

The Great Movie Ride: One of the most loved classic movies of all time is *The Wizard of Oz*. It would only seem appropriate there would be a classic Hidden Mickey to accompany the scene.

Look closely at some of the flower groupings in the scene. They form classic Hidden Mickey shapes.

A classic Mickey can also be found in The Wizard of Oz *tribute at the top of the trees, midway along the mural, on the back wall of the show scene.*

👍 **The Hollywood Brown Derby:** One of the signature trademarks of the original Los Angeles restaurant was a collection of caricatures of some of Hollywood's most famous celebrities and dignitaries. Keeping with tradition, the Park's version of this classic also features its own collection of drawings. As you enter the restaurant, locate the far left wall across from the podium for a historical, if not hidden, Mickey.

A caricature of Jimmie Dodd, wearing Mouse ears, resides on the wall. Dodd was known as the leader and "Head Mouseketeer" on the 1950s television program the Mickey Mouse Club.

✌ **Mickey's of Hollywood:** Take a look at the canopy that extends over the windows of this shop.

There is a smiling Mickey head on the front portion of the canopy.

👉 **Mickey's of Hollywood:** Similar to the Emporium found on Main Street, U.S.A., this shop serves as the Park's main merchandise location and features three-dimensional representations of Mickey in some of his more famous roles. Look for other Hidden Mickeys in the product racks, and on poles and bins throughout the place.

MICKEYS is also spelled out on four vertical dividers, two on each side of the store, separating the sections of the shop.

👍 **Park entrance:** Observe here, upon entering Disney's Hollywood Studios, a collection of references to Mickey.

Look for Mickey heads on trash cans, directional signs, three-dimensional figures, store windows, clapboard signs, and entrance signs throughout Disney's Hollywood Studios.

👏 **Sid Cahuenga's One-of-a-Kind Antiques and Curios Shop:** The former shop now currently serves as a Guest Information Center specializing in handling My Disney Experience, for MyMagic+, and FastPass+ concerns. On the porch of this former shop is a Dalmatian to the left of the entrance doors.

A black classic Hidden Mickey spot is on the Dalmatian's left hind leg.

Star Tours—The Adventures Continue: This attraction takes Guests on a wild ride across the galaxy, as droids C-3PO and R2-D2 attempt to safely return a Rebel spy to the Rebel Alliance. The first reference to Mickey can be found in a large tree that supports an upper platform in the Ewok Village queue area.

The Hidden Mickey can be clearly seen in the top portion of the tree.

Star Tours—The Adventures Continue: Once you enter the main hangar building, C-3PO is standing in front of a StarSpeeder preparing to do some diagnostic checks on the flight vehicle.

If you look at the monitor in front of C-3PO, there are two circles and a large half circle that form a classic Hidden Mickey.

👍 **Star Tours—The Adventures Continue:** Further into the queue area, there is a droid who is inspecting luggage and personal objects. There are three pieces of luggage that feature Mickey references.

One shows a Sorcerer's Apprentice hat. Another one features a Mickey plush. And finally, the last reflects a set of Mouse ears inside a piece of luggage.

A REAL TUFFY **Star Tours—The Adventures Continue:** As you continue up the ramp, there is a series of silhouettes that feature Star Wars-inspired passengers about to board.

Wait for an Astromech droid, looking like R2-D2, to pause for a moment and reveal antennas that form a classic Hidden Mickey.

👋 **Star Tours— The Adventures Continue:** There are several references to Hidden Mickeys in the various locations Guests visit while experiencing their Star Tours journey. Because of the attraction's nature and the number of different locations available to Guests, no two adventures seem to be the same.

Look for one just when you begin your journey. This sequence features Darth Vader attempting to stop the StarSpeeder 1000 vehicle in an effort to capture the Rebel spy. In the background there is a Stormtrooper donning a set of Mouse ears.

During your turbulent excursion through Coruscant, there is a sign in the planet's native language that spells out MICKEY. The sign is near the tunnel where the StarSpeeder 1000 goes in the wrong direction through the busy sky highways.

At another locale on Coruscant, after your StarSpeeder 1000 crash-lands on the platform and is lowered below into the hangar, look for four recessed panels in the top half of the back wall of the structure. Each panel has a classic Hidden Mickey on it.

👉 **Tatooine Traders:** This store, which is named after the home planet of Luke Skywalker of the Star Wars films, is a unique gift shop, where one who goes in search of Hidden Mickeys will soon come across a Build-Your-Own Lightsaber display near the shop's exit.

On the far right lower counter, you'll see a classic Hidden Mickey emerge thanks to bursts of blue lights that form a perfect Mickey head.

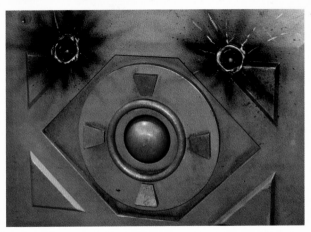

SUNSET BOULEVARD

The Hollywood Tower Hotel, once an elegant and lively hotel, serves as the backdrop for The Twilight Zone Tower of Terror attraction at the end of Sunset Boulevard. The hotel is said to have closed October 31, 1939, after lightning struck the building and caused the elevator bays, along with five people, to mysteriously vanish.

Fantasmic!: In this nighttime spectacular, you'll uncover numerous Hidden Mickey shapes in the projection portion of the show. According to the story line, Mickey's imagination gets the best of him and during one sequence there is a collage of Disney characters that appears in the water and in the dancing fountains.

Look for all the characters to surface in bubbles at the start of the show. There are several instances where the bubbles gather to form a perfect Hidden Mickey. For example, images of the White Rabbit, Dopey, and Pinocchio form a perfect Hidden Mickey shape.

Legends of Hollywood: There is a ticket window that marks the entrance to this store. Look closely on the counter.

Some very old coins have been placed together to form a classic Hidden Mickey.

Once Upon a Time: The Hidden Mickey at this shop is in the scrollwork above the property's door.

The Hidden Mickey can be viewed from inside the shop, above the doorframe as you leave.

Rock 'n' Roller Coaster Starring Aerosmith: At the entrance to this steel roller coaster attraction, riders will gaze upon a large mural featuring the members of Aerosmith. The mural also features a collection of Hidden Mickey images.

The young boy in the front seat of the car is wearing a set of Mouse ears.

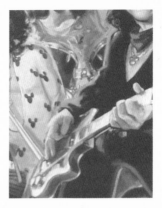

Lead singer Steven Tyler's shirt is covered with Mickey heads. Band member Joe Perry is wearing a black suit; around his neck is some bling forming the shape of a Hidden Mickey.

👉 **Rock 'n' Roller Coaster Starring Aerosmith:** As you enter the lobby for G-Force Records and find yourself in the entrance queue (and after you reach the inner room and walk past the tile floor), look down at the carpet.

The queue features a collection of distorted images of Mickey's head throughout the carpet.

 Rock 'n' Roller Coaster Starring Aerosmith: Here is a very difficult Hidden Mickey to find even for the most advanced spotters. Just before you enter the preshow area, look for a poster that reads **COSMIC CAR SHOW**. The poster features a very tiny Mickey head at the bottom portion of the poster.

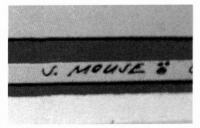

It is under the front tire of the car. The Mickey image is at the end of the signature of J. MOUSE.

👍 **Rock 'n' Roller Coaster Starring Aerosmith:** Look for this next Hidden Mickey image in the preshow area where we meet the band members.

A classic Hidden Mickey is formed by three coils of wire placed on the floor in front of the sound board, where Aerosmith's members are standing.

A REAL TUFFY **Rock 'n' Roller Coaster Starring Aerosmith:** There is a Hidden Mickey image on the rear license plate of each limo ride vehicle.

The year sticker in the upper right corner of each license plate forms a classic Hidden Mickey.

👍 **Rock 'n' Roller Coaster Starring Aerosmith:** As you wait to board your limousine, there is a collage of pictures on the wall to your left in the standby side of the queue.

Look for a collection of Mickey-inspired stickers on the board.

👉 **Rock 'n' Roller Coaster Starring Aerosmith:** As you exit the attraction, just prior to entering the shop, there are rows of boxes apparently used by the band during their tours. Search for the one labeled **BOX #15.**

It will be on your right as you exit. The "o" in BOX forms a classic Hidden Mickey.

👆 **Rock 'n' Roller Coaster Starring Aerosmith:** Once you enter the shop, head toward the back counter.

There's a Hidden Mickey and a Hidden Minnie comprised of guitar picks on the farthest checkout counter at the back of the gift shop.

There are also several guitar picks that have been arranged in circles to form a classic Hidden Mickey on the wall behind the glass at one end of the shop. The Hidden Mickey is surrounded by a series of pictures featuring members of the band.

👆 **Rock 'n' Roller Coaster Starring Aerosmith:** On one wall in the store, near the photo purchase area, look for a speaker system and additional band equipment that references Mickey Mouse.

The looped wires of the speaker have been arranged in the shape of a Hidden Mickey.

👆 **Rock 'n' Roller Coaster Starring Aerosmith:** As you exit the building, look to your right; there is a radio-themed food stand featuring the call letters KRNR and the words THE ROCK STATION.

Right in the letter "R" in THE ROCK STATION, you should eye a classic Hidden Mickey.

👍 **Sunset Ranch Market:** "Meet me at Third and Fairfax" became a common refrain during the golden days of Hollywood. It was used to tell friends and acquaintances to meet at the original Farmers Market. In the Park's version of this California landmark, look for Rosie's All-American Café.

A REAL TUFFY *There is a Mickey sticker in the bottom corner of the display case near the window where you pick up your food.*

There is also a reference to Mickey on a military emblem that reads AIRCRAFT WORKER *on the eatery's back wall.*

🚋 **The Trolley Car Café:** This location serves as the new home for Starbucks. On the building's exterior facing Sunset Boulevard, look for a date on the top of the building. While not a traditional Hidden Mickey, the date is significant.

The year 1928 is a direct reference to the year Mickey Mouse was introduced to animated film fans.

The Twilight Zone Tower of Terror: The hotel library is not only home to books, but also the hotel's collection of antiques and exotic curiosities, an old television set, and various *Twilight Zone* replicas. Can you locate a song sheet on the shelf of a bookcase?

The song sheet reads WHAT! NO MICKEY? WHAT KIND OF PARTY IS THIS?

 The Twilight Zone Tower of Terror: At the first stop on the ride, the ghostly images of the hotel's five permanent Guests appear.

The little girl in that group is still holding her Mickey Mouse doll.

The Twilight Zone Tower of Terror: As you exit the attraction, you'll discover that you are in the hotel's basement. Suddenly you'll come upon a cage with various gadgets and equipment. See if you can spot a collection of gauges.

The gauges are located to the left of the cage and form a classic Hidden Mickey.

The Twilight Zone Tower of Terror: Just past the cage there is a photo pick-up counter. Look to your left prior to entering the attraction's merchandise shop.

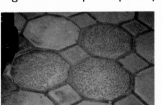

The tiles are discolored just enough to form a classic Hidden Mickey.

PIXAR PLACE

Serving as one of the Park's main icons is the Earffel Tower, a 130-foot-high water tower similar to those that once dominated the landscape of the old-time movie studios. It sits just behind this area of the Park and sports a set of Mouse ears (with a hefty hat size of $342\,{}^{3}/_{8}$).

👉 **Animation Gallery:** Look for the window that features the name of this store.

It shows Mickey Mouse sitting down at a drawing table ready to sketch.

👉 **Disney Junior—Live on Stage!:** Look for a collection of Mickey references, some more obvious

than others, throughout the building that houses this interactive stage show.

Speaker units, showtime boards, and the signs all have Hidden Mickeys.

👉 **Popcorn cart:** There is a small alcove across from Toy Story Midway Mania! that features a popcorn cart and drinks. There are several Hidden Mickey gems that reside within this location.

On the large popcorn box to the right of the cart, there is a kernel of popped popcorn that forms the perfect profile of a Mickey head.

👉 **Popcorn cart:** Once you discover the popcorn box, turn to the back of the stand; up on the back wall

there you'll see a collection of plates featuring the members of the Toy Story gang.

The plates feature a series of images on them, including a Mickey head.

👍 **Toy Story Midway Mania!:** Inspired by the series of Disney • Pixar films, this interactive 4-D adventure is bursting with Hidden Mickeys throughout the attraction and queue area. Look for your first Hidden Mickey on the far wall, just prior to collecting your 3-D glasses.

The Mickey head is painted on the wall of the standby line right before those in line ascend the steps of the queue area.

🐟 **Toy Story Midway Mania!:** Look for the large picture of Mr. Potato Head, Slinky, and Bullseye. The three are each pictured in their own circle and the three shapes, when merged, form a perfect Hidden Mickey.

The image of the three Toy Story characters is on the wall directly behind the left load area for the attraction.

👆 **Toy Story Midway Mania!:** In the mini-game "Rex and Trixie's Dino Darts," look for a long-necked dinosaur holding his own Hidden Mickey.

The dinosaur is actually holding three balloons that form a perfect Hidden Mickey.

👍 **Toy Story Midway Mania!:** Look for another Hidden Mickey in "Rex and Trixie's Dino Darts."

Look for the volcano in the sequence. Directly below the mountain is an image of Mickey's head.

👆 **Toy Story Midway Mania!:** See if you can spot the dot in the exclamation point after CIRCUS FUN! as you travel from the last game to the screen where your score is tallied.

The dot forms a classic Hidden Mickey.

 Toy Story Midway Mania!: A classic Hidden Mickey is located in the eye of the chicken you should see as you exit the attraction.

The Hidden Mickey is on the spine of the Tin Toy book at the attraction's exit. It is on the second chicken down from the top of the book's spine.

☞ **Voyage of The Little Mermaid:** This theatrical adventure, which combines live actors and puppets with special effects, has two Hidden Mickeys. The first is in the marquee that marks the entrance. Observe the bubbles, which are floating slightly above the evil sea witch Ursula's hand.

Three bubbles form a classic Hidden Mickey.

👍 **Voyage of The Little Mermaid:** In the waiting area near the theater's entrance, there is a framed picture of a world map on the far wall.

Images of the globe conveniently form the shape of Mickey.

STREETS OF AMERICA

Sci-Fi Dine-In Theater Restaurant, a cornerstone of this part of the Park, is inspired by the drive-in movie craze of the late 1950s and early 1960s, when nearly four thousand of these establishments were the place to be in the United States. Today only a handful of these venues still exist, and **Disney's Hollywood Studios** is home to our own version from a bygone era.

👉 **It's a Wonderful Shop:** *It's a Wonderful Life,* the classic 1946 picture starring James Stewart and Donna Reed, is the driving force behind this holiday-themed shop. Those who enter the shop, which is between Pizza Planet and Mama Melrose's Ristorante Italiano, will find that it features a Hidden Mickey immediately inside, to the right.

> *Find a Christmas tree in the corner with three ornaments forming the classic Mickey head shape.*

👉 **Lights, Motors, Action! Extreme Stunt Show:** This nonstop motor adventure combines some high-octane stunts while revealing special effect secrets along the way. The show also includes a collection of Hidden Mickey shapes.

> *On the house on the left side of the stage, the bottom of the rock wall features a Hidden Mickey.*

> *There is a Mickey hidden on the bell in the bell tower.*

> *On occasion, and depending on wind conditions at showtime, there is a Hidden Mickey to look for in the final jump sequence. It can be seen in the center stage area of the production.*

> *Finally, in the motorcycle shop's window, top right side, there is a Hidden Mickey formed by the placement of some old gears.*

👉 **Mama Melrose's Ristorante Italiano:** Three distinct Hidden Mickeys are featured in this Italian restaurant. You don't have to travel far within the restaurant to spot them (though you might be hard-pressed to depart once you've entered). The three Hidden Mickey shapes are actually just inside the area of the restaurant where Guests check in.

There is a statue of a Dalmatian, and on his right shoulder is a black spot in the shape of Mickey's head.

On the upper right portion of the wall behind the podium,

there is a distorted image of Mickey's head created in plaster.

A REAL TUFFY *There are grapes and leaves woven into the latticework just to the right of the podium. One of the leaves forms a perfect Hidden Mickey.*

👉 **Muppet★Vision 3D:** All of the fun and mischief associated with the Muppets come to life during this 3-D adventure. But, before you enter the theater, see if you can spot the Hidden Mickey in the outside

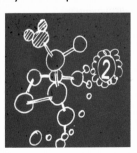

queue area on a poster along the side of the building. It is also home to the *Frozen* character queue.

The poster reads 5 REASONS, and in the bottom left corner is a classic Hidden Mickey.

👍 **Muppet★Vision 3D:** Once inside the preshow area, concentrate on the television monitors for your next two Hidden Mickeys. During the first part of the preshow on the video monitors, a test pattern appears after you see the words VIDEO DISPLAY TEST.

The black test lines form a classic Hidden Mickey on the white background.

👎 **Muppet★Vision 3D:** During the main 3-D film, there are several Hidden Mickey references at the conclusion of the film.

There are fireworks that go off on the screen and one forms the shape of Mickey.

 Muppet★Vision 3D: There is also an explosion that goes off during the film and it apparently blows out the back of the theater. Kermit the Frog enters on a fire truck while bystanders look in.

People in the crowd don Mouse ears and carry Mickey shaped balloons. Interestingly, there is also an emblem of Cinderella Castle on the back of the fire truck.

👆 **Muppet★Vision 3D fountain:** Locate the Muppet-inspired fountain outside of Muppet★Vision 3D, and observe the object on which Gonzo is standing.

The small float Gonzo balances on resembles Mickey Mouse's head.

👍 **On the grounds:** Check the splatters of paint that lie everywhere between and around the two buildings that house the Stage 1 Company Store and Muppet★Vision 3D.

Look on the ground in this area and you will discover several Hidden Mickeys.

👉 **Pizza Planet:** This quick-service eatery, which takes its name from the pizzeria in the Toy Story animated films, features three Hidden Mickey shapes. The first two are on the wall above the podiums where Guests place their orders.

There is a constellation of stars on the left side and the right side of the large mural; the stars from each group form a Mickey head.

👉 **Pizza Planet:** There is also a Hidden Mickey on the far left wall of this establishment.

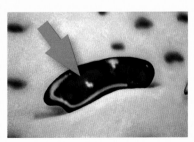

A Mickey head is hidden appropriately on a slice of pepperoni.

👆 **Sci-Fi Dine-In Theater Restaurant:** Across from the check-in podium, over to your right, there is a window cabinet with papers pinned to the wall.

There is a small Mickey image behind the glass.

Now, turn your attention back to the check-in podium, on the back side of the movie screen; there is a classic Hidden Mickey on the wood wall.

👆 **Sci-Fi Dine-In Theater Restaurant:** Once you enter the main restaurant floor, several "parked" cars await to provide Guests the opportunity to relive a drive-in experience while enjoying a meal in front of a big screen. Look for a wooden fence at the back of the restaurant; just above the wall there is a series of trees.

One tree forms a perfect Hidden Mickey.

A REAL TUFFY **Sci-Fi Dine-In Theater Restaurant:** There is also an abstract Hidden Mickey cleverly hidden in the tile, above the far right door of the restaurant's kitchen.

It is very difficult to distinguish, but there is a definite side profile of Mickey that can be spotted among the small tile blocks.

Stage 1 Company Store: This shop, home for everything Muppets, is located at the exit to Muppet★Vision 3D. It is also the location for two Hidden Mickey shapes; one is on a bookcase within a series of paint splatters.

Three circular turquoise splatters form the classic Hidden Mickey.

 Stage 1 Company Store: Next, look up at the clothesline that extends from the Happiness Hotel to spy a pair of Mickey's shorts.

It's not clear if these were the same pair that were used by Rizzo the Rat during the Muppet★Vision 3D preshow sequence. After all, there is also a set of Donald Duck's clothes hanging up here, too. (In the preshow, prankster Gonzo tells Sam the Eagle that he would like to introduce the audience to a special guest: Mickey Mouse. Then Rizzo the Rat, in a Mickey costume, comes onstage. As a frustrated Sam the Eagle chases Gonzo offstage, Gonzo mentions that he also has Donald Duck waiting backstage.)

A REAL TUFFY **Streets of America mural:** There is a mural at the end of San Francisco Street featuring newspapers hanging from a picture of a newsstand.

There are copies from a 1928 paper that feature references to the industry's first animated cartoon with synchronized sound: Steamboat Willie.

👍 **Streets of America mural:** While on the main thoroughfare of the Streets of America, look for a sign that reads VENTURE TRAVEL AGENCY. There you will find a multitude of Mickey images.

Inside the agency's window, there is merchandise, postcards, a picture of the Disney ships, a picture of Walt and his wife, Lillian, holding a Mickey plush, and several other salutes to Mickey and his friends.

👍 **Streets of America mural:** On the far left bottom corner of the large New York mural, there are the words RON NEW YORK. Look to the left of those words and see if you can spot a set of golf clubs in the picture.

Behind the set of golf clubs is a picture of a sand trap in the shape of Mickey; it's similar to the design of one at the sixth hole at Disney World's Magnolia Golf Course.

Streets of America mural: In one of the side streets there is a barbershop. See if you can spot the Dalmatian sign marking the address number as 1.

There is a classic Mickey formed by three of the spots on the dog's left shoulder.

Writer's Stop: In the middle of the shop there is a counter that features Mickey-themed towels, magnets, and a clipboard. There is also a book on the shelf featuring a classic Hidden Mickey on the spine.

Look for a book with a map-themed jacket and globes that form Mouse ears.

133

DISNEY'S
ANIMAL KINGDOM
THEME PARK

ENTRANCE PLAZA, THE OASIS, DISCOVERY ISLAND

Encounter a land of exotic animals and adventures at one of the largest animal theme parks in the world. Discovery Island, the entrance to the themed areas, was originally dubbed "Genesis" to signify the starting point on your journey. The Park's icon, the Tree of Life, stands at its center and rises to nearly 145 feet tall.

👉 **Disney Outfitters:** This shop is located near the base of the Tree of Life, and can be easily spotted by Guests who are heading toward DinoLand U.S.A. In one of the store's side rooms, known as the Constellation Room, there are stars clustered together that form what on closer inspection look like various animal shapes.

Look up over the doorframe in the Constellation Room and see if you can spot the dolphin-shaped star assemblage: there is a classic Hidden Mickey among those stars.

👍 **Entrance Plaza, Rainforest Cafe:** Standing at the Park's approach is this signature themed restaurant known for being, "A wild place to shop and eat!" On the sign featured at the entrance is a classic Hidden Mickey.

The Hidden Mickey is on the neck of Iggy, the wise iguana.

A REAL TUFFY **Island Mercantile:** Located across from Disney Outfitters is this perfectly themed shopping venue. See if you can spot the Hidden Mickey along the back wall on a post.

*Can you connect the dots? This Hidden Mickey
is a constellation of yellow spots within
a honeycomb cell atop a column.*

A REAL TUFFY **It's Tough to be a Bug!** This 3-D spectacular examines the world of bugs—from the perspective of those that either slither, glide, crawl, and fly (or all of the above). It is also home to a classic Hidden Mickey. But you'll need the help of a Cast Member to locate this elusive shape. Once inside the theater waiting area, go to your far left. This is actually the lane designated for those using wheelchairs and scooters.

*On the far left wall, about six feet from the
ground, there is a classic Hidden Mickey in the
rockwork of the structure. Given the dark
conditions of the theater and the waiting area,
you may need to shine a light on the Hidden
Mickey to get a better look.*

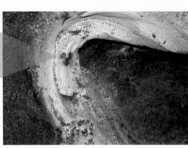

👆 **Pizzafari:** Pizza is king at this Oasis eatery located on the walkway that heads toward the Park's Africa area. Inside the restaurant are six themed rooms featuring creatures of every size, species, and shape. In the room closest to the front walkway entrance, look to your left at the colorful leaves painted on the wall up toward the ceiling.

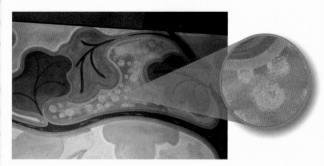

Tucked under the red leaf are three whitish spots that form a classic Hidden Mickey.

👆 **Pizzafari:** In that same room, there is also a small alcove painted with a mural that features possums and hanging bats.

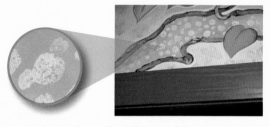

Look closely on the left side of the mural among an array of green and orange leaves for the classic Hidden Mickey formed by three whitish spots.

👍 **Pizzafari:** In one room just beyond the counter where you order your food, there are paintings of sea life on the walls. Look for the turtle on the far wall.

Check out the spots along the bottom portion of his shell. Three spots form a great Hidden Mickey.

 Pizzafari: In one of the back rooms of the restaurant, there is an image of a leopard.

Look closely at the spots on the leopard. There are several on and around the leopard that form classic Hidden Mickey shapes.

A REAL TUFFY **Tree of Life:** The tree, which features approximately 325 carved animals in its base and trunk, serves as the host structure of the It's Tough to be a Bug! 3-D theater show. There is an upside-down classic Hidden Mickey above the eye of the carved hippopotamus.

The hippopotamus is visible from the pathway and bridge that connects the two themed areas of Africa and Asia.

Tree of Life: By featuring more than 103,000 translucent leaves, the tree is extremely realistic, even down to the green moss that surrounds portions of the trunk. See if you can spot the bison on the front of the tree when entering the Park.

A classic Hidden Mickey is made up of green moss and is next to the sculptured image of the bison.

AFRICA

The mystery and beauty of this continent come alive in a variety of attractions and live shows all designed to showcase the delicate balance of nature and humans. Kilimanjaro Safaris is perhaps the most unique attraction at the Walt Disney World Resort because no two journeys—or wildlife encounters—are ever the same.

👆 **Dawa Bar:** This bar and refreshment refuge sits on the main walkway of the themed area and is home to its own Hidden Mickey shape. Look on the front side of the bar.

There are three screws that are arranged to form a perfect Hidden Mickey.

👆 **Festival of the Lion King:**
Inspired by the 1994 Disney animated feature *The Lion King*, this stage-show spectacular also has its own Hidden Mickey. At the point in the show where the floats start to come out, look for Timon's float. Around the base on the bottom of the float are a number of painted symbols.

Among these images are defined circles that form a classic Hidden Mickey shape.

👆 **Harambe Market:** There is a small covered seating area located in the marketplace; anything brewing on one of the pillars?

There is wall art featuring an image of Mickey Mouse sipping a cup of morning coffee.

👆 **Harambe Market:** In the back section of the marketplace, Guests will find African-inspired clothing, artifacts, and native goods. See if you can spot the shield with the three circles that form a classic Hidden Mickey.

Look for a shield with a circular top; at the bottom, on a red background, the Hidden Mickey has a white head and black ears.

👍 **Harambe Market:** There is a unique image of Mickey found on the outside wall to the marketplace. Look for the word FICHWA!

Just above the writing, there is an image of Mickey Mouse.

As a bonus, there is also a Hidden Donald located on the outside wall, visible as you enter the Harambe train station while aboard the Wildlife Express *on your return trip to Africa.*

🐾 **Kilimanjaro Safaris:** In the queue area of the attraction, look for the sign which describes cheetahs.

A close look at the tail of this majestic creature will reveal a classic Hidden Mickey.

A REAL TUFFY

Kilimanjaro Safaris: The second Hidden Mickey is found during the safari adventure and the journey across the famed Serengeti.

Easiest to see when viewed from above, Flamingo Island is shaped like Mickey's head.

👉 **Mombasa Marketplace:** On the outside of this shop, look for a round utility cover. You will discover your next Hidden Mickey.

Surrounding the utility cover is a collection of pebbles embedded in the cement that combine with the utility cover to form a perfect Mickey head.

👍 **On the grounds:** Look for this Hidden Mickey on the walkway situated between Rafiki's Planet Watch and Kilimanjaro Safaris behind a food market location.

In the surface of the cement, there is a large Hidden Mickey in the shape of the famous mouse's head.

Pangani Forest Exploration Trail: Formerly known as Gorilla Falls Exploration Trail, this self-guided walking tour allows Guests to explore the remote jungles of Africa. The name Pangani was used in the 1998 Disney film *Mighty Joe Young*. Upon reaching the Research Center building, check out a backpack that's hanging on the wall.

Look very carefully at the backpack for a small emblem of a Mickey head on the left side of the bag.

Rafiki's Planet Watch, Affection Section: Housed in the back section of Conservation Station is a unique petting zoo for kids of all ages. It is home to two Hidden Mickey designs on a seasonal basis.

At various points throughout the year, two Olde English babydoll Southdown sheep named Pearl and Swan are groomed and shaved with a Mickey head shorn into the wool on their backside.

Rafiki's Planet Watch, Conservation Station: As Guests enter the building that houses Conservation Station, they are treated to an amazing mural inside and around all the walls of the facility. There are literally hundreds and hundreds of animals depicted on  the mural. Plus, there are more than a hundred Hidden Mickey images tucked away in the mural, residing everywhere—on the animals themselves to the habitats depicted throughout the mural.

Given the complexity and the magnitude of the mural, it would be impossible to list the entire collection. Enjoy some of our favorite photos—and have fun with your own hunting!

👍 **Rafiki's Planet Watch, Conservation Station:**
As soon as you enter the main building, there is a sign with panels that change every few seconds to create a new image. Wait for the orange sea star to appear.

See if you can spot the side profile of Mickey in the center of the creature.

👈 **Rafiki's Planet Watch, Conservation Station:** Inside the main building, there are viewing windows, where veterinary scientists are on hand to provide research and education. When you look into the surgical center, see if you can spot a classic Hidden Mickey.

On the far wall of the surgical center are three black nets that are hanging in such a way that they form a classic Hidden Mickey.

👉 **Rafiki's Planet Watch, Conservation Station:** Can you spot the microplates that are on the windowsill of the viewing windows of the Science Center's research and education center?

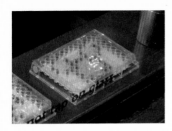

Find the set of microplates that feature a chemical substance in certain holes depicting a perfect Hidden Mickey.

👍 **Rafiki's Planet Watch, Conservation Station:** There are trees scattered throughout the main building. Some are bunched together, however. Can you spot the Hidden Mickey around the base of the trees in close proximity to one another?

The grates at the bottom of each tree have a repeating Hidden Mickey pattern.

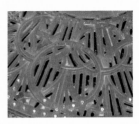

✌ **Rafiki's Planet Watch, Conservation Station:** There is a section here that is known as the Song of the Rainforest area, and hidden throughout the various murals of this pavilion are Hidden Mickey shapes that come in every size.

On the bottom of one of the panels is a set of wild mushrooms that form a classic Hidden Mickey.

On the panel to the far left of the display is a very tiny Hidden Mickey; it's on the back of a fly!

A REAL TUFFY *On the right front side of the tree which contains the cockroach display, look for a long vine of red berries. The three berries at the very bottom of the vine resemble a classic Hidden Mickey.*

On the front panel where the cockroach display is located, there is a brownish butterfly that has a very tiny Hidden Mickey on its back, right where the two wings meet.

As you step inside the Song of the Rainforest display, there is a classic full body profile of Mickey on the back tree.

Look for the mural of Grandmother Willow from the 1995 Disney animated feature Pocahontas. *On a branch by her on the bottom right side is a beautiful Hidden Mickey profile.*

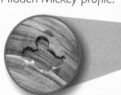

Seek out the one panel featuring a tree limb below the Song of the Rainforest sign, which displays a perfect Hidden Mickey on its bark.

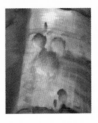

A REAL TUFFY Look for the panel that extends across the one side of the mural and see if you can spot the collection of small red flowers and the one that specifically features a yellow Hidden Mickey head on its petals.

👉 **Rafiki's Planet Watch, Harambe Train Station:** Access to Rafiki's Planet Watch is only available through the beautifully themed train system that connects it to Africa. Before you embark on your journey, take a look upward to see if you can spot your first Hidden Mickey.

There are crossbeams in the rafters of the station that feature a collection of classic Hidden Mickeys.

👆 **Rafiki's Planet Watch, *Wildlife Express*:** While aboard this line's Eastern Star Railway train, try finding any "signs" of Mickey throughout your journey.

During your journey back and forth on the rails, there are directional signs along the way in the shape of Mickey's head. The protected areas where the safari animals go to sleep at night also feature informational signs about their habitat environments.

🐾 **Tamu Tamu Refreshments:** Just across from Harambe Market is this place, where one can take a break and look for another round utility cover to discover your next Hidden Mickey.

On the walkway that connects Africa and Asia, this Hidden Mickey is formed by pebbles embedded in the cement around the utility cover, similar to the Hidden Mickey in Mombasa Marketplace.

👉 **Tamu Tamu Refreshments:** The covered seating area here also features a Hidden Mickey. But first locate Baloo, the bear from the 1967 Disney animated feature *The Jungle Book*, on the sidewall of the covered seating area behind this fast-food establishment.

Once you discover the whereabouts of Baloo, look directly above him to see a distorted image of Mickey Mouse in plaster.

👍 **Tusker House Restaurant:** Once inside the restaurant, walk into a small dining room located on the left side of the facility.

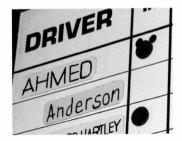

A classic Hidden Mickey is drawn on the fictitious attendance board on the wall to your left. It's next to the top name, AHMED, on the board.

👍 **Water closets:** On the second-story loft, just above the water closets and restrooms, which are situated between Tamu Tamu and the Mombasa Marketplace, is a classic Hidden Mickey.

There is a rounded basket with two large circular pieces of fruit. The fruit and basket resemble a perfect Hidden Mickey.

ASIA

The Himalayas are the setting for a thrill-packed speeding-train adventure and your chance encounter with the legendary Yeti. Nearby, a self-guided tour of a Southeast Asia temple offers an up-close look at the mighty Bengal tiger, cotton pygmy geese, fruit bats, a flying fox, and a Komodo dragon.

Expedition Everest—Legend of the Forbidden Mountain: Inside the queue area for the attraction is a supply store known as Tashi's Trek and Tongba Shop. Stocking mountaineering equipment, this shop is a necessary stop for all would-be adventurers. In the one case, next to the shirts on display, is a collection of Yeti dolls.

One of the Yeti dolls in the case is wearing a small set of Mouse ears.

 Expedition Everest—Legend of the Forbidden Mountain: Within the queue area, is a section referred to as the Yeti Museum. It includes a campsite setup that's stocked with gear and a tent. Concentrate on the lantern at the campsite exhibit.

Take notice of the three dented areas on the base of the lamp. They form a classic Hidden Mickey.

 Expedition Everest—Legend of the Forbidden Mountain: In the load area, peek at the back wall of the building you just exited. The exterior wall features a carved wood motif.

Within this swirly pattern, there's an image that resembles a classic Hidden Mickey.

 Expedition Everest— Legend of the Forbidden Mountain: In the area where passengers unload, look to the right of the moving vehicle and on the side of some rocks.

Hidden very carefully within the rock formation is a perfect Mickey head that's settled in the grassy brush.

🐾 **Flights of Wonder:** Education is key to this interactive adventure about the winged creatures of the animal world. Within the attraction, the Caravan Stage draws the most attention, but peer over to a rounded building and tower on the right side.

Featured in the stonework of the building along two repeating panels are a series of Hidden Mickey shapes.

🐾 **Kali River Rapids:** This river-raft ride takes Guests on a thrilling tour through a lush jungle landscape that's been partially ravaged by illegal logging. It is also home to a Hidden Mickey.

In the first building that Guests enter in the queue area, track down a collection of pots and pans hanging on a wall. Three pots are arranged in such a way that they form a perfect Hidden Mickey.

👍 **Maharajah Jungle Trek:** Several Hidden Mickey images are lurking within the four wall murals of former maharajahs located in this attraction's tiger overlook. The first set of Hidden Mickeys is located on the first image on your right as you enter the temple ruins and archway.

In the mural, look at the earrings worn by the former great leader. They resemble a perfect Hidden Mickey shape. There is also a small Hidden Mickey on the corner of the maharajah's jacket.

👈 **Maharajah Jungle Trek:** The second set of Hidden Mickeys is located on the image opposite the first image cited, on your left as you enter the temple ruins and archway.

Look again at the earrings worn by the former prince. They, too, resemble a perfect Hidden Mickey. There is also a small Mickey just below the wrist of the former leader as he extends his bow and arrow.

 A REAL TUFFY **Maharajah Jungle Trek:** At the other end of the archway there are two more murals, each with a maharajah. Concentrate on the great king in the right-hand mural as you are about to exit the temple ruins and archway and spot the cloud formation.

Above the maharajah in the mural are puffy blue clouds. Three of the clouds form a perfect Hidden Mickey.

👉 **Maharajah Jungle Trek:** On the left side, just as you are about to exit the temple ruins and archway, look toward the mountain range to the left of the former king.

On the left mural, there's a small classic Mickey in a brown rock formation tucked away on the left side of the mountain range.

A REAL TUFFY **Yak & Yeti Restaurant:** The restaurant is comprised of a series of rooms. In the one room immediately to your left and around the corner is your next Hidden Mickey. Look for three canisters hanging from a shelf for what initially may not look like a Hidden Mickey unless you're viewing it at the correct angle.

If you peer up from underneath to view the canisters, you'll see that they form a classic Hidden Mickey.

DINOLAND U.S.A.

This salute to classic American roadside towns of the 1940s came about when some amateur fossil hunters found dinosaur bones in 1947. After scientists bought the dig-site, dino-themed businesses began to sprout up in the area. Industrious paleontology students converted their living and research quarters into Restaurantosaurus, Chester and Hester transformed their gas station into a souvenir shop—and built a Jurassic carnival—and the Dino Institute started to give tours.

👉 **The Boneyard:** As the story goes, this impressive dig site was established by the Dino Institute to sponsor further exploration of and education on dinosaurs. Proceed up to the second floor and see if you can spot an archeology display behind this cage. Look closely on the top of the table inside the archeology display.

> *There are three coins that form a classic Hidden Mickey on the table.*

The Boneyard: Now, cross the bridge over to the dig site and see if you can spot a similar cage featuring an archeology display. Look for the fan inside the cage with the brand name ZERO.

> *On one of the blades of the fan, there is a tiny image of a Mickey head.*

A REAL TUFFY **The Boneyard:** A journey back over the bridge to the entrance will lead you to your next Hidden Mickey.

> *On the bridge, embedded in the cement, are three stones, which form a classic Hidden Mickey.*

👍 **The Boneyard:** Look closely at the water fountain immediately to your left, as you enter the play area.

There is a showerhead above the water fountain featuring three holes, which form a classic Hidden Mickey.

👆 **Chester & Hester's Dinosaur Treasures:** This onetime gas station has taken on a new life and is now your exclusive stop for all dinosaur-related souvenirs. Inside, near the middle of the shop, look up to spot a Hidden Mickey.

The famous mouse is hanging from a post in marionette form.

👆 **Cretaceous Trail:** This children's play area features a large dinosaur known as a Pachycephalosaurus.

You can find a Hidden Mickey on the back of the playful dinosaur!

👍 **Cretaceous Trail:** Next to the Pachycephalosaurus, there is a set of paint cans on top of an easel.

The three paint cans form a nice classic Hidden Mickey.

DINOSAUR: The action never stops on this scary, prehistoric tour aboard a rip-roaring Time Rover vehicle that's designed to help Guests save a dinosaur from extinction. As you enter the attraction, there is a mural that explores one of the many theories explaining the extinction of the dinosaur.

Look for a set of Mickey ears in the mural featuring the reddish explosion cloud. The mural is repeated in the large circular room where Guests gather prior to entering the attraction.

DINOSAUR: Just inside the preshow area, once you enter the building, look for a picture of a tree on your right side. There are two classic Hidden Mickeys in the mural. One is near that tree and the other is on it.

The first is on the tree trunk, across from a lower right branch. The second is featured in the mossy region next to the tree.

DINOSAUR: This Hidden Mickey comes up rather quickly on the attraction.

Once in your Time Rover, look for a dry-erase board that will be to the left of your moving vehicle (and featuring a Mickey head on it).

DINOSAUR: The Time Rover journey introduces Guests to one of the most viscous dinosaurs that roamed the land, the Carnotaurus.

See if you can spot the friendly Hidden Mickey on the top portion of this dinosaur's head.

DINOSAUR: Just when you thought you've seen enough of the Carnotaurus, check out the mural of one in the photo purchase part of the store tied to the attraction.

This Hidden Mickey is located on the bottom part of the neck of the Carnotaurus.

Finding Nemo—The Musical: There are several small signs just outside the theater featuring showtimes for the musical adventure.

On the bottom right corner of each sign there is a Hidden Mickey made out of bubbles.

A REAL TUFFY **Horned dinosaur:** Across from Chester & Hester's Dinosaur Treasures is this replica of a horned dinosaur that's actually made from recycled materials.

On the horned dinosaur's left side, there is a gold Steamboat Willie *Cast Member pin. It is located on the fourth dorsal plate on the dinosaur's back. The* Steamboat Willie *pin is given to all Cast Members who achieve one year of service with the company.*

👍 **Primeval Whirl:** Climb aboard this swirly-twirly, time machine adventure and attempt to observe "obvious" Hidden Mickeys on the meteors hurtling by throughout your journey.

The meteors feature surface craters that form the classic Hidden Mickey shape.

Dinoland U.S.A.

🦕 **TriceraTop Spin:** Marking the entrance to this kid-filled attraction is a baby Triceratops, which is balancing a red-and-yellow-striped ball on its horns.

A classic Hidden Mickey can be found on the scales of the baby Triceratops's right side, directly under his first horn.

👉 **TriceraTop Spin:** Across from TriceraTop Spin, to the left of the photo op location, and to the right of the horned dinosaur, look for a classic Hidden Mickey.

The Hidden Mickey can be found in the cement at the front of the second parking space between the horned dinosaur and the photo op location.

167

REST OF
THE RESORT

WATER PARKS

According to a legend, Blizzard Beach was created when a freak snowstorm led to the opening of Florida's first ski resort. Naturally, the snow did not last long, but the waterlogged ski jumps it left behind were ideal for fun in the sun. The story of Typhoon Lagoon tells of a colossal storm that hit Mount Mayday, leaving in its wake an oasis complete with a giant wave pool, lazy river, and coral reef.

DISNEY'S BLIZZARD BEACH

A REAL TUFFY **Cross Country Creek:** Experience the lazy-hazy days of summer every day on this half-mile-plus journey on an inner tube around Blizzard Beach. During your journey, see if you can spot an image of Mickey in rock form along the facing of a stone bridge.

In fact, the Hidden Mickey appears to be wearing a sorcerer's hat.

👉 **Teamboat Springs:** Jump aboard and enjoy one of the world's largest white-water–raft rides. As you approach the exit to the attraction, you'll be treated to a perfect Hidden Mickey.

There is a fun representation of Mickey's head made from three inner tubes from the Park's attractions.

DISNEY'S TYPHOON LAGOON

 Castaway Creek: While you drift on an inner tube and enjoy this two-thousand-foot-long lazy river ride that encircles the water park, you may discover a few Hidden Mickeys along your journey toward the back of the Park, below the shipwrecked *Miss Tilly*. As you meander along the shoreline, stay vigilant—several abandoned nautical items have been left behind.

First, look for a set of cannonballs that have been conveniently placed together to form a perfect Hidden Mickey.

Next, in that same general area close to the cannonballs, there is also a depression in the rock that resembles Mickey.

A REAL TUFFY **Castaway Creek:** Before you leave the area, cast your eyes upon a walkway that parallels the river ride. Along that walkway, there's one more opportunity to make an impression with your fellow Hidden Mickey hunter!

The image of Mickey is again in depressed-rock form. It is directly across from the cannonballs and the first depression in the rocks we revealed to you.

👉 **Crush 'n' Gusher:** One of the Park's signature attractions is this roller coaster–like raft ride. Before you begin your adventure, take a moment to look for two Hidden Mickeys that are on the premises. The

first is in the queue area, where Guests gather prior to ascending the staircase or elevator.

One is a temperature gauge that resembles a Hidden Mickey.

👉 **Crush 'n' Gusher:** Look for the second once you arrive at the top of the staircase, just near the elevator doors.

A collection of circles here are designed to resemble Mickey.

👍 **Ketchakiddee Creek:** Find Mickey in a small cave in this themed area that's devoted to pint-sized Guests and the nautical and splish-splashing adventures that await them.

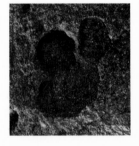

An impression of Mickey is located on top of the rock wall.

Miss Tilly **bridge:** There are several bridges that connect the various themed areas of Typhoon Lagoon. On the bridge leading to the Typhoon Lagoon Surf Pool, look for a perfect Hidden Mickey.

See if you can spot the plank with one end cut in the shape of Mickey's head.

A REAL TUFFY **On the grounds:** It would be shocking for any fan of Hidden Mickeys to miss this example of the famous mouse scattered throughout the Typhoon Lagoon Surf Pool and beach areas!

Notice a collection of lightning rods that each sport a three-dimensional Mickey head on top.

On the grounds: Water is the name of the game at Typhoon Lagoon, but every once in a while you have to take the time to quench your thirst! When you do, check out several of the drinking fountains scattered throughout the Park.

There is a cutout shaped like Mickey's head on one side of the box-shaped base for each drinking fountain.

Shark Reef: This Hidden Mickey is a fun one to spot for any scavenger hunter. Pay attention to the side of the capsized ship.

Find a grouping of barnacles that form a classic Hidden Mickey.

👍 **Singapore Sal's:** This establishment carries everything you could possibly need for sunbathing, swimming, and snorkeling. It also possesses a couple of classic Hidden Mickeys. Just make sure you have time to spare for this first salute to the famous mouse.

Three nautical themed wall clocks are positioned upside down. Together, they form a perfect Hidden Mickey.

Singapore Sal's: There are several painted images of Mickey's head scattered throughout the shop.

The images of Mickey's head are all in white paint, and they are featured on the various boxes and crates that shore up the shop's theme.

Storm Slides: Get ready for a big splash as a trio of winding, water-gushing slides catapult you on a watery and sensational descent. Now, take a moment and examine the steps of the wooden bridge approaching the top of the slide.

The wooden bridge is just past a small boat and a sign that reads JUST MARRIED. The end of one of the planks has been cut to resemble Mickey's ears.

MINIATURE GOLF

As the story goes, Santa was flying back to the North Pole one Christmas Eve and discovered snow over Florida. He decided to make the location a vacation site for his faithful elves with two distinctly different eighteen-hole golf courses—thus constructing Winter Summerland Miniature Golf. Fantasia Gardens also features two eighteen-hole courses, both themed to Disney's 1940 classic film *Fantasia*.

FANTASIA GARDENS AND FAIRWAYS MINIATURE GOLF

👉 **"Dance of the Hours"–themed hole:** The music of Amilcare Ponchielli provided the inspiration for the musical segment "Dance of the Hours" in the 1940 Disney animated feature *Fantasia*. The Disney interpretation of this musical piece also introduced audiences to two classic characters: Hyacinth Hippo and Ben Ali Gator. Here, the pair provides the setting for a classic Hidden Mickey.

Look for the Hidden Mickey situated under the statue of Ben Ali Gator holding Hyacinth Hippo in the air.

👍 **Starting tee:** Guests, as well as Hidden Mickey hunters, will enjoy this continued salute to Mickey throughout the course.

Mickey's head is featured as the starting tee for each hole of this unique golf course.

WINTER SUMMERLAND MINIATURE GOLF

☞ **Starter Shack:** There are two Hidden Mickeys on the front side of the building.

If you are standing and facing Santa's sled, there is one on the left and one on the right side.

☞ **Starter Shack:** There are also two Hidden Mickeys on the back side of the building.

One is situated above the water fountains, and the other is by the merchandise area.

👆 **Winnebago:** This classic motor home makes for the perfect vehicle to begin your golf adventure. And, while you are at it, look for the three Hidden Mickeys tucked carefully around this vintage trailer.

> *Two Hidden Mickeys are located on the side of the Winnebago that's nearest to the restrooms.*
>
> *The third is on the merchandise side of the trailer.*

👋 **Winter golf course:** What Christmas celebration would not be complete without a decorative tree. In fact, the beautiful Christmas tree near the end of the course is also the home to three Mickeys.

The Mickeys are all decorations and are situated among the other hundred, or so, festive ornaments. Each is formed by a glittery ball with ears, in the colors of red, gold, and silver.

👆 **Winter golf course:** The sixteenth hole features Santa slipping down the chimney. Right before you tee up, check out the Hidden Mickey above the fireplace mantel.

A wreath hanging above the fireplace includes a traditional-looking Hidden Mickey designed to resemble a Christmas ornament.

A REAL TUFFY Winter golf course: There is also a Hidden Mickey draped along the garland, once again above the fireplace at the sixteenth hole.

Mickey makes a very cute gingerbread man that can be found in the garland above the fireplace mantel

👍 **Winter and Summer golf courses:** Just before you wrap up your game of miniature golf, look for this pretty Hidden Mickey near the eighteenth hole!

The Hidden Mickey is located above the eighteenth hole and is featured in the garland that wraps around the building.

MAGIC KINGDOM RESORT AREA

With the introduction of the Magic Kingdom came a collection of themed resorts. Walt Disney believed these resorts should support and become extensions of the various themed lands of the Magic Kingdom. That is why the placement of these unique resorts was so critical. For example, Disney's Contemporary Resort is the closest themed resort to Tomorrowland. Disney's Polynesian Village supports Adventureland, while Disney's Fort Wilderness Resort and Campground is associated with Frontierland. The later addition of Disney's Grand Floridian Resort & Spa became the perfect themed extension to Main Street, U.S.A.

DISNEY'S CONTEMPORARY RESORT

👉 **Bayview Gifts:**
Be sure to look
down as you enter
this fourth-floor
shop, known as
B.V.G. for short. You
don't want to miss
the Hidden Mickey,

which is located in the colorful carpet design.

👍 **California Grill:** This restaurant is known for its
magnificent views of the Walt Disney World Resort
property. If you peer out the center window toward

the Magic Kingdom, you'll
see some familiar
landscaping.

*Look at the main entrance to
see a circular garden planted
to resemble the face of your
favorite mouse.*

👉 **Chef Mickey's:** In this fun-filled dining experience,
a multitude of obvious Mickey images can be found

scattered throughout the
restaurant, from the playful
to the decorative. The
mouse is featured on
canisters, cookware,
cookbooks, pictures, three-
dimensional figures, plates,
and more. Here are a couple
of the more subtle ones.

As you wait to enter the restaurant, check out the pillar that features Hidden Mickeys toward the bottom.

A favorite photo op location at the restaurant features a three-dimensional Mickey holding a bowl and ladle.

Contempo Café: While you enjoy your meal, be sure to check out the chairs that fill the seating area of the establishment.

The back of each chair features a Hidden Mickey cutout.

Entrance: Find the Walt Disney World Security kiosk.

On the top portion of the structure you'll see a classic Mickey head.

Fantasia Market: Around the corner from the B.V.G. shop is the Fantasia Market, which incorporates Mickey's shape into its various fixtures.

Look at the sides of the metal shelving units for three circles that align to form Mickey's head and ears.

Fantasia Shop: This shop features a special set of Mouse ears that dominate the front and back entrances.

There are also bins throughout the store depicting a perfect Mickey head on them.

The Game Station arcade: Have fun finding the bursts of Mickey shapes hidden on the carpet.

Mickey is at the center of a few starburst patterns.

Grand Canyon Concourse mural, designed by Mary Blair: Among the many unique features of this massive southwest-themed mural is a five-legged goat, which is found on the monorail-facing side. In addition, on that same side, peer diagonally down from the five-legged goat to see a colorful blue and yellow tree.

The top of the tree features one blue circle and two yellow circles, which make up this upside-down Mickey head.

A REAL TUFFY **Grand Canyon Concourse mural, designed by Mary Blair:** On the mural just opposite the monorail track is a friendly owl located twenty feet up from the fourth-floor concourse.

A Hidden Mickey can be spotted on its wing.

 Grand Canyon Concourse mural, designed by Mary Blair: On the side of the mural adjacent to the Contempo Café, located on the far right bottom corner, is a Native American girl.

Look for a Mickey shape on the front of her skirt.

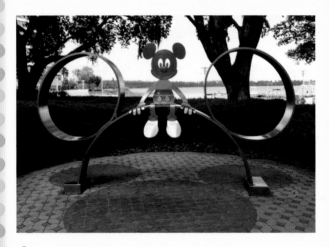

👍 **On the grounds:** Head out the back toward the resort's main pool and look for a silver-colored sculpture featuring Mickey sitting playfully on top of a set of Mouse ears.

> *Located beneath that same set of Mouse ears is also another classic Hidden Mickey head, this time in the black cement on the ground.*

👈 **On the grounds:** Look for several jogging route signs scattered throughout the resort's property.

Catch a running Mickey on the sign.

A REAL TUFFY **On the grounds:** Head toward the outside steps, those leading in the direction of the Transportation and Ticket Center. Another silver-colored Mickey cutout sits atop the Service Building for the resort.

This Hidden Mickey is difficult to spot, and you have to be on the fifth-floor staircase or above to see our favorite mouse.

👉 **The Sand Bar:**
Look for this quick-service restaurant located adjacent to the resort's main pool area. This restaurant features three **Hidden Mickeys.**

The first Hidden Mickey is located on the wall of the facility. Try to find a classic Hidden Mickey lurking near the nautical flags.

A second Hidden Mickey is also featured holding signal flags, this time at the back door of the restaurant.

And finally, a Hidden Mickey is featured not as an image but as the word "M-I-C-K-E-Y," which is written out in nautical flags on the front window of The Sand Bar.

BAY LAKE TOWER AT DISNEY'S CONTEMPORARY RESORT

👍 **Footbridge:** A stroll over to Bay Lake Tower from the Contemporary's fourth-floor Grand Canyon Concourse takes you along a walkway bridging both locations.

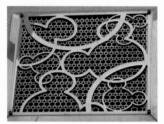

Along this walkway try and find a speaker unit featuring a classic Mickey in its grillwork.

 Lobby, atrium: Be sure to look up at the chandeliers.

If viewed from the proper angle, the round shapes form a Hidden Mickey.

✌ **Lobby, hallways:** Anything familiar about the etching on the elevator doors?

Beautiful Mickey designs are fashioned into the mirrored patterns.

✌ **Lobby, hallways:** Each floor of Bay Lake Tower features a collection of contemporary paintings, and in nearly every picture you will discover classic Hidden Mickey shapes.

In one example, where Donald Duck is superimposed on top of a grid of circles, a trick of the eye makes you think a classic Hidden Mickey is superimposed on top of Donald.

👆 **Lobby, hallways:** Hallway carpets also feature beautifully crafted Hidden Mickey shapes in them.

Look at the darkest blue and medium blue areas to follow purposely positioned circles.

👍 **Pool:** Look to the resort pool slide's blue metal tower to spot some familiar silhouettes.

The pool slide tower features a classic Hidden Mickey shape on its sides and at the opening of the slide.

193

DISNEY'S POLYNESIAN VILLAGE RESORT

👉 **BouTiki merchandise shop:** Once inside this first-floor shop, locate three large statues, which are scattered throughout this location.

On the back of each statue, you'll find a classic Hidden Mickey.

👍 **Kona Café:** Originally known as the Coral Isle Cafe, this uniquely styled restaurant features a collection of Hidden Mickeys throughout the place. For example, at the podium, gaze up at the Kona Café's sign to spot a Hidden Mickey.

It is located on the top right portion of the sign.

👈 **Kona Café:** Next, check out the colorful carpet and find Mickey hidden throughout the restaurant when you look down.

Look at the center of the tropical flower design.

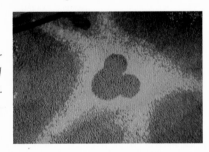

 Kona Café/lobby atrium: Look straight toward the lobby atrium and notice the large balls hanging from the rafters of the Great Ceremonial House.

A careful positioning and a discerning eye will help one capture a Hidden Mickey. The ropes holding the large balls in place also feature Hidden Mickeys on them.

 A REAL TUFFY **Kona Island Coffee Bar:** A beautiful Hidden Mickey can be found in the countertop tile work.

Facing the cash register, look at the tiled countertop just to the right.

 Main lobby: Go inside the Great Ceremonial House, from the front doors of the resort. Look down.

A Hidden Mickey welcomes you from within the pattern in the marble floor.

Main lobby: Take the elevator to the second floor of the Great Ceremonial House and check out the Polynesian-themed painting to the right as you wait.

There are Mickey shapes carefully hidden within the painting. Possibly, it was just a happy accident, but still it's a great collection of Hidden Mickeys nonetheless.

Moana Mercantile: Can you find a Hidden Mickey positioned on a high shelf ledge within the shop?

It is formed by combining three blue and green glass balls that are knotted together with rope.

DISNEY'S GRAND FLORIDIAN RESORT & SPA

👉 **Cítricos:** Two Hidden Mickeys can be found inside this beautifully themed restaurant.

One is located on the door to the wine cellar and chef's table.

The second is found on the pillar in front of the open kitchen. Three hanging pots form a classic Hidden Mickey shape.

👍 **Convention Center lobby:** A short walk from the resort's main building takes you to the Convention Center. Once inside, head toward the main atrium and look up.

A Mickey balloon is featured in the impressive mural. Plus, similar to the outline of the resort, there are resort towers that also feature weather

vanes with the classic Hidden Mickey in their designs.

✊ **Convention Center lobby:** There are also Hidden Mickey shapes in the carpet of this part of the resort.

Look for Mickey at the center of a gold fleur de lis–like pattern in the carpet, just near the pink, gold, and green striping.

👉 **Grand Floridian Cafe:** Not to be outdone by the Convention Center's look, Hidden Mickeys abound and can also be found throughout this restaurant's carpet design.

Look at a white design on a red stripe in this carpet's motif.

👉 **M. Mouse Mercantile:** The resort's main gift shop features a familiar-looking mouse on the shop's sign.

Look for the three-dimensional Hidden Mickey.

👉 **Main lobby:** Stepping into Disney's Grand Floridian Resort & Spa is like taking a step back in time. Among its many Victorian-inspired features are marble floors that dominate the lobby. And scattered throughout the marble floors of the lobby area are Disney classic characters.

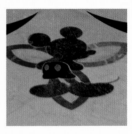

Mickey Mouse and the rest of the fab five (Minnie, Goofy, Pluto, and Donald) can be seen at the lobby entrance.

👉 **Main lobby:** Marble floors on the first floor of the resort feature more classic Hidden Mickey designs in them.

At a square corner, an orange-marble outline of Mickey stands out against a green background.

👉 **Main lobby:** Elegant Hidden Mickey shapes can also be found on the lobby's carpet.

There are areas in the carpet that feature majestic red and gold Mickey head scroll designs.

👉 **Main lobby:** Look for a collection of Hidden Mickey shapes that dominate the wallpaper at the resort.

There are Hidden Mickey patterns throughout on the wallpaper.

👉 **1900 Park Fare Restaurant:** Full-body representations of Mickey and Minnie emblematize the entrance's marble floor.

The playful pair is just past the podium.

👍 **On the grounds:** Before you enter Disney's Grand Floridian Resort, peer upward and take a peek at the weather vanes on some of the resort buildings.

A classic Hidden Mickey can be found on weather vanes throughout the resort.

✌ **On the grounds:** The luggage carts that transport Guests and their bags throughout the resort grounds have Hidden Mickeys on them.

Each vehicle sports the familiar three-circle cutout design.

👉 **Pool:** Look toward the top of the main pool area.

There you will discover a rock formation exposing a cleverly cutout Hidden Mickey.

A REAL TUFFY **Victoria and Albert's:** Inside the elegant confines of this award-winning restaurant, just past the podium and just before you enter the formal dining area, is a single, beautiful Hidden Mickey.

Find it within the carpet next to the door. The gold lines of ears don't fully close above the head.

THE VILLAS AT DISNEY'S GRAND FLORIDIAN RESORT & SPA

👍 **Main lobby:** Located on the main floor of the Villas, near the elevators, are iron gates that decorate the atrium area.

Fashioned in the bottom of each gate are designs reminiscent of Mickey's general shape.

👆 **Main lobby:** Classic Hidden Mickeys can be found on the floor of the Villas in the carpet design.

The Mickeys form a circle within an orange-and-gold Victorian lacy pattern.

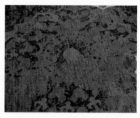

👆 **Main lobby:** On the first floor of the Villas is a map of the resort property; you'll notice it on the left side as you enter the main building.

The map features a collection of Hidden Mickey designs as trees scattered throughout the property.

👍 **On the grounds:** There are covered walkways that lead Guests to the pool and main resort building.

The decorative white latticework features Mickey shapes. A similar design can also be found on the outside of the building which houses the Villas.

DISNEY'S WILDERNESS LODGE RESORT

Artist Point: Two Mickeys are hidden inside this rustic-themed restaurant. The ceiling of the large room is decorated by a Western-style mural.

On the left shoulder of the one Native American in this work is a classic Hidden Mickey.

Artist Point: Look at the wall leading to the small dining room, which also features a mural.

In the line of trees, find the classic Hidden Mickey.

Hallways: There are several light covers throughout the hallways of the resort.

If you look closely, you will discover a Hidden Mickey cleverly tucked away among the rocks.

Hallways: Hidden Mickey designs are scattered throughout the resort, and can be found on the wooden floor planks and columns that characterize the property.

The Hidden Mickeys here have a more subtle effect since they are formed from a dark stain on the wood.

👆 **Hallways:** Disney's Wilderness Lodge Resort has hallway carpets which feature Hidden Mickey shapes in them.

The Mickey heads are blue on a thin gold strip.

👈 **Main entrance:** Look for a sign that reads BEAR CROSSING.

The sign features a cutout of Mickey and Humphrey the bear.

 Main entrance: Look very carefully at the black cement of the resort's porte cocheres.

On the black stripe closest to the steps that lead Guests to the parking lot, there is a tiny classic Mickey traced in the cement.

A REAL TUFFY **Main entrance:** As you walk up the steps from the parking lot toward the resort, look at the support beams on your left-hand side.

A partially blocked Hidden Mickey is covered by a black metal band that extends around the beam. Only the top of Mickey's head is visible, along with a portion of his ears.

👆 **Main lobby:** Can you guess who is driving the bus featured on the Walt Disney World Transportation sign in the lobby of the resort?

Mickey Mouse shares a ride on the resort's bus sign.

👆 **Main lobby:** Behind the resort's front desk on the back wall is a set of keys.

On the set of keys is a classic Mickey head.

👆 **Main lobby:** At the far left corner of the resort is an eighty-two-foot-tall fireplace resembling the rock strata of the Grand Canyon. Face the fireplace and look to the terra-cotta–colored rocks that are level with the second floor's wooden beams.

A subtle impression of Mickey is embossed into the rock just near the outward-facing wooden beam off to the right.

👉 **On the grounds:** If you exit the back of the resort and head toward the Teton Boat & Bike Rentals complex, look to the far right corner of the main building.

A classic Hidden Mickey is etched into the wooden beam of the building. The Mickey is located on the right side of the beam about four floors up from the ground.

👆 **On the grounds:** Downstream from Fire Rock Geyser in the shallow stream is a slightly distorted Hidden Mickey.

Rocks form the popular mouse's head and ears.

👆 **Pool:** Located at the children's play and pool area is a small waterslide supported by a collection of logs.

The ends of three logs form the shape of a Hidden Mickey.

👉 **Roaring Fork:** On the wall at the entrance to this quick-service location is a shadow box featuring a collection of fishing and tackle gear.

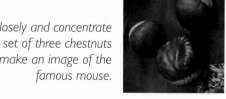

Look closely and concentrate on a set of three chestnuts that make an image of the famous mouse.

👍 **Security gate:** Find the Walt Disney World Security kiosk. The structure resembles a small log cabin.

On the column closest to the security door is a small Hidden Mickey carved into the pillar.

✌ **Territory Lounge:** On the large map marking the entrance to the lounge area is a themed painting on the left wall.

Look for a piece of Native American-inspired pottery that features a classic Hidden Mickey.

 Territory Lounge: Take a look at the ceiling mural to discover a group of horses.

On the backside of one caramel-colored horse is a clever Hidden Mickey shape.

 Whispering Canyon Cafe: At a fireplace in the rear room of this restaurant, bend down low and look for a classic Mickey cutout on the outer grillwork.

It's the third icon from the left corner along the bottom row of icons.

THE VILLAS AT DISNEY'S WILDERNESS LODGE RESORT

👉 **Hallways:** Throughout the hallways of the resort there are Hidden Mickeys in the décor.

Look up to the ceiling, and in the decorative framework of the hallway are Hidden Mickey designs on each side.

👍 **Main lobby:** Once inside the resort, look immediately to your right and spot a map of the United States titled, "Scenic Line of the West."

You will discover several images of Mickey in different locations on the map.

👆 **Main lobby:** In a small room to the right of the lobby, there's a train-inspired picture with people in a field of flowers. Look for two Hidden Mickeys within the image as well as one on the frame itself.

In the river there are clusters of mossy rocks that form a classic-looking Hidden Mickey. Interestingly, to the right of the river and to the left of the train, there are three gray rocks in an open field that also resemble a Mickey head.

Then concentrate on the corners of the frame and you will discover a gold Mickey head.

A REAL TUFFY **Main lobby:** There is a small room to the right of the entrance. It is identified by the Carolwood Pacific Railroad train and gaming tables.

Once you spot the fireplace, look on the left side of the hearth and you will see a classic Hidden Mickey embedded into the stonework.

Main lobby: A classic Hidden Mickey can be found in the rockwork in the main lobby of the resort.

It's on the last stone pillar at the main entrance of the Villas, approximately three feet off the ground, on the side of the pillar facing the entrance.

A REAL TUFFY **Main lobby:** Another classic Hidden Mickey is also located on each side of the first-floor elevators in the Villas main lobby.

Each is carved into the wooden panels that decorate the resort walls. The one on the right is situated between a themed-framed portrait and the elevator doors. The other is tucked behind a canvas banner that hangs from the wall.

 Main lobby: In the main atrium of the Villas are crossbeams that extend out from the corners of the resort lobby. The top portion of the beam features a carved snake on top.

The beam itself is located to the right of the atrium fireplace and features a tiny three-dimensional Mickey in one of its knots. He is just sitting inside the knot and smiling at anyone who may pass by.

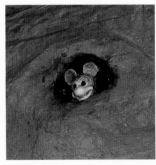

Main lobby: The fireplace to the left of the beam also features a playful Hidden Mickey. The hearth features cast-iron, three-dimensional forms of animals on the grillwork of the fireplace.

On the back of the turtle is a classic Hidden Mickey.

Main lobby: Look for this elusive Hidden Mickey directly above the fireplace in the main atrium.

A profile of Mickey's head is about twelve feet from the ground, surrounded by small red shapes.

Main lobby: To the left of the entrance doors, just past the elevators, a dark, classic Mickey can be found on the baseboard near the hall carpet.

It's down the hallway on your right, about eight to ten feet before you reach Room 1507.

On the grounds: A short walk will take you from Disney's Wilderness Lodge Resort to the Villas at Disney's Wilderness Lodge. Under the covered walkway, you can find a **CAUTION BIKE CROSSING** sign on a post.

The sign features a cutout Mickey in wrought iron.

DISNEY'S FORT WILDERNESS RESORT AND CAMPGROUND

 Main lobby: Once inside, look above the front desk and spot three horseshoes that have been placed carefully to form a classic Hidden Mickey.

They are attached to a crate immediately above the sign reading REGISTRATION CHECK IN/OUT.

A REAL TUFFY **Main lobby:** A playful Hidden Mickey can be seen inside one of the light posts near the door by the registration lobby.

The light is just to the right of a window with a pamphlet stand in front of it.

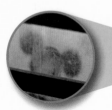 **Mickey's Backyard BBQ:** Take a stroll to this fun-packed eatery and you will see several Hidden Mickey shapes.

They are all located on the stage, in the backdrop mural. See if you can spot Mickey's famous head on the body of one of the farm animals, in the wood pile, and on the side of the barn.

👆 **Mickey's Backyard BBQ:** Featured on the restaurant's sign is a classic image of Mickey in traditional frontiersman gear holding a banjo.

While not quite hidden, it's most certainly a charmingly classic rendering.

👉 **On the grounds:** Near the bus depot, look for the sign for the Tri Circle D Ranch trail rides.

Two classic Mickey designs are on the sign, with a "D" in the center of them for the name of the facility.

On the grounds: Look down as you enter the resort check-in facility and spot a patch of grass and flowers.

You will discover two sets of three smooth rocks strategically placed together to form a classic Mickey head.

👉 **On the grounds:** Next to Pioneer Hall, home of the Hoop-Dee-Doo Musical Revue, is the Tri Circle D Ranch, which possesses a collection of Hidden Mickey shapes that dominate the grounds.

You can spot Mickey on signs, buildings, fence posts, and gates.

👍 **On the grounds:** Adjacent to the Tri Circle D Ranch is the blacksmith barn.

Branded on the blacksmith sign at each end of the barn is a classic Hidden Mickey.

👉 **On the grounds:** The stable across the way from the blacksmith barn is the home of the Walt Disney World Resort horses.

Be sure to step into the stable house to see the beautiful horse's bridle on display inside a glass case. The Mickey design on the bridle is reminiscent of the original design used when the resort initially opened.

👉 **On the grounds:** The home of the Walt Disney World Resort horses is also the location of the musical calliope, which is enclosed behind glass.

Check out the bale of hay to the right of the carriage to catch three horseshoes that are connected together to form a classic Hidden Mickey.

👍 **Trail's End Restaurant:** Take a bus ride to the next stop on your Hidden Mickey journey.

Located on the front porch at the restaurant is a checkerboard with two small barrel stools. On the top of each stool is a classic Mickey head.

👉 **Trail's End Restaurant:** Venture inside the restaurant to spot a collection of skillet pans.

Three pans are strategically hung together to form a classic Mickey head behind the buffet counter.

A REAL TUFFY Trail's End Restaurant: Look very carefully across from the restaurant and see if you can find a classic Hidden Mickey embedded in the ground.

Mickey is about twenty feet from the porch.

EPCOT RESORT AREA

With the opening of Epcot came a dramatic expansion of the resorts for the Walt Disney World property. Prior to the opening of Epcot, the Disney resorts that existed throughout the property were confined to the Magic Kingdom area. The first resort to test the waters and expand beyond that region was Disney's Caribbean Beach Resort, opening in 1988. Later additions, including Disney's Beach Club Resort, Disney's Yacht Club Resort, and Disney's BoardWalk Resort, soon became the places for Guests wishing to spend their day at Epcot, situating them a boat ride or a short walk away from the Park.

DISNEY'S CARIBBEAN BEACH RESORT

👉 **Marina:** Look for a lighthouse on the grounds of the resort. It is situated to the right of the main pool area and behind the building known as Old Port Royale.

On the sign that reads BAREFOOT BAY BOATYARD is a classic Hidden Mickey.

 On the grounds: If you're walking from the Trinidad North building and heading toward Old Port Royale, look down at the sidewalk.

Once you approach a fence surrounding the pool area and are near a pathway leading to the parking lot, there is a small Hidden Mickey head embedded in the concrete on the walkway.

👍 **Pool:** A pirate ship dominates the children's water play area at the resort.

Once there, concentrate on the helm of the ship, near the wheel, and you will spot a classic Hidden Mickey.

👉 **Pool:** The resort's main pool area is appropriately themed to resemble a Spanish-style fort that's reminiscent of those scattered throughout the Caribbean.

On the back wall of the pool area adjacent to the pool slide is a large, almost distorted looking, Hidden Mickey on the side of the themed fortress.

DISNEY'S BEACH CLUB RESORT

👉 **Ariel's:** There was once a beautifully themed restaurant named Ariel's. As time went by, however, this restaurant changed and became more of a facility that holds special events.

On the walls farthest away from the entrance, there is a portrait featuring a classic Hidden Mickey in it. The painting features a mermaid; there is also a collection of coral that forms a classic Hidden Mickey.

👆 **Beach Club Marketplace:** Once you're inside this establishment, but prior to walking down the small flight of stairs, you'll see a picture whose frame features a gold Hidden Mickey in the bottom portion of it.

The Mickey is just to the left of the bottom right-hand corner.

👆 **Beach Club Marketplace:** Anything familiar about those sand dollars in the carpet?

These Hidden Mickeys— three sand dollars connected together— dominate the carpet design.

👉 **Beaches & Cream Soda Shop:** This perfectly themed restaurant is a great example of a fun place to eat at the Walt Disney World Resort and features two classic Hidden Mickey designs. Look for the first one on the hamburger press used by the chefs.

In fact, you will discover a few of these presses in the vicinity of the restaurant's stove.

Beaches & Cream Soda Shop: There is also a classic Hidden Mickey formed by three onion rings in the mural above the restaurant's seating area chart.

Look for a red-and-white striped bag with the onion rings spilling out, right next to a set of music notes.

 Cape May Cafe: A classic Hidden Mickey is featured on the wall as you enter the restaurant.

The Mickey is featured on a plate that sits on a decorative shelf on the wall of the restaurant.

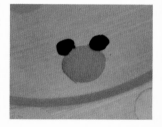

Hallways: In the hallways look down at the beautifully themed carpet.

You will discover Hidden Mickey shapes delicately woven into the design and fabric as seashells, bubbles, and beach balls.

Hallways: A close examination of the hallway wallpaper will also reveal classic Hidden Mickey shapes throughout.

Look directly below each seashell for a perfect Mickey that's centered in the coral design.

👍 **Hallways:** Look for the inside walkway, which wraps around the Cape May Cafe.

A small figurine of Mickey Mouse is standing inside a shadow box, which houses a sand castle.

🐚 **Hallways:** A painting hangs in a hallway near the back entrance to Cape May Cafe.

The painting is of Florida and gold classic Hidden Mickey heads are featured in the corners of the painting. There are also Hidden Mickey shapes in the top portion of the painting. These red-shaped Mickey heads are tucked into the shell-like images on the top of the painting.

A REAL TUFFY Main lobby: Off to the right of the lobby, as you head toward the Beach Club Marketplace, carefully examine the marble floor.

A very tiny Hidden Mickey is etched into the tile and surrounded by a circle.

DISNEY'S BEACH CLUB VILLAS

👉 **Hallways:** There is a beautiful mural of an early-turn-of-the-twentieth-century seaside resort featured on the wall of the breezeway as you walk in from the quiet pool of the Villas.

The picture includes a combination of Hidden Mickey designs, from a railing pattern featuring everyone's favorite mouse to a classic Mickey in the sand and a large Mickey balloon.

👆 **Hallways:** The hallways of the Villas also feature classic Hidden Mickey shapes patterned into the carpet.

A particularly enchanting one is formed by flower vines.

 Hallways: At the Villas, head toward the bathrooms off the lobby inside the entrance doors.

On the left wall in the side hallway is a picture titled Cape May. Look at the top border and you'll spot a train just to the left of center of the picture. A classic Hidden Mickey can be seen in the coal car just behind the engine.

👉 **On the grounds:** There is a beautiful Ariel statue that dominates the entrance to the Villas.

At the bottom of the statue are three seashells that form a classic Hidden Mickey.

👉 **Solarium:** Across from the Ariel statue is this place, which is situated between the resort and villas. Along the hallway of the Solarium are various portraits depicting life and what it was like at the turn of the twentieth century. Featured in each of these pictures is an array of Hidden Mickey images and designs. Try and find the following in each of the paintings:

Mickey-themed balloons.

Mickey on some spare tires.

Some car hood ornaments with Mickey heads.

Mickey on the funnel stack of a Disney ship.

A beach towel with Mickey.

A cloud that features Mickey's face.

Finally, everyone's favorite mouse is shown sitting in a tree and on the peak of a building, both above a small building with a brown roof.

DISNEY'S YACHT CLUB RESORT

👍 **Hallways:** There is a beautiful collection of nautical-themed carpets featuring Hidden Mickey shapes in them in the hallways of the resort.

👈 **Main lobby:** A large globe serves as the centerpiece of the entrance to the resort.

There is a classic Hidden Mickey located near Antarctica, off the coast of Africa. The blue-colored Mickey head is also located near a playful sea serpent on the colorful globe.

👇 **Main lobby:** In a seating area across from the registration desk of the resort, there is an array of decorative nautical cabinets.

On one cabinet, the drawers have been labeled with the following names: Mickey, Minnie, Donald, Daisy, Goofy, and Huey.

Main lobby: In the lobby area of Disney's Yacht Club Resort, Guests are greeted by an eye-catching nautical-themed carpet that dominates the area.

Featured throughout the carpet are Hidden Mickey designs.

Yachtsman Steakhouse: In 1986, a unique cow was born in Edgerton, Minnesota. What made her so unique were her natural spots in the form of Mickey's head. In 1998, The Walt Disney Company contacted the family that owned the cow and invited her to spend her time at the resort. The cow relocated to Mickey's Starland in the Magic Kingdom at Grandma Duck's Farm. Over the years, Minnie Moo, as she was called, took up several other residences, including at the Tri Circle D Ranch at Disney's Fort Wilderness Resort and Campground. In 2001, Minnie Moo passed away.

As a tribute to Minnie Moo, there is a picture of her at the inside entrance to the restaurant.

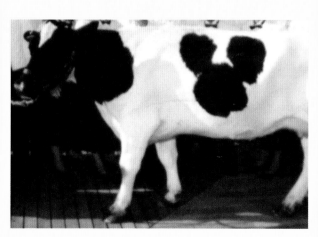

DISNEY'S BOARDWALK RESORT

 Atlantic Dance Hall: Inside the main room of this property's special dance hall, there is a classic Hidden Mickey deftly placed into the large painting on the wall right of the stage.

One large swirly shape serves as the head and two smaller ones act as the ears.

A REAL TUFFY **Flying Fish Café:** Inside the restaurant on the left-side mural above the sitting area is a set of Mouse ears cleverly hidden within the picture near the image of the roller coaster car.

Find them just to the right of the word RIDING.

Hallways: There are also Mickey designs in the carpet throughout the hallways and in the elevators.

A particular subtle design features six gold Mickeys encased in a heart shape with a floral oval.

Hallways: Heading toward the elevators on the Villas side of the resort, take note of the lamps lighting the way.

Mickey designs are etched into the light fixtures.

A REAL TUFFY **Main lobby:** Find the beautiful miniature working carousel, a tribute to those rides that used to dominate the New Jersey shoreline—the inspiration for the resort. A closer examination of the delicately painted horses will reveal four with classic Hidden Mickeys on them.

The horses with the Mickey shapes tend to be white horses with familiar brown spots.

A REAL TUFFY **Main lobby:** Behind and above the registration desk are beautiful murals highlighting some of Disney's most famous castles, from Sleeping Beauty and Cinderella to the one in *Beauty and the Beast*.

In the tree line in front of the Beast's castle is a collection of trees that form classic Hidden Mickey shapes.

Main lobby: Located in this area of the resort are several period-themed armchairs bearing shapes that form a mouselike silhouette.

The three gold berries stand out the most, but there are also three blue berries and an arrangement of three blue flowers that all remind seekers of Mickey's shape.

Main lobby: Spot the floral designs in the carpets in this part of the resort featuring Hidden Mickey shapes in them.

A pink ribbon in the corner of one carpet forms a particularly perfect Mickey head.

A REAL TUFFY **Main lobby:** In 1881, a six-story, elephant-shaped hotel was built in Margate, New Jersey, just outside of Atlantic City. As a tribute to Lucy, as she was affectionately called, there is a representation of this pronounced pachyderm in the resort's main lobby.

On the red-colored latticework in the canopy situated atop Lucy, a classic Hidden Mickey design can be found.

Main lobby: An elegant lobby lamp tops them all with a Mickey.

When entering from the main driveway entrance and reaching the merhorse chandelier, turn left to find a gold Mickey atop the lampshade.

Pool: At the main pool area, across from the Kiester Coaster waterslide, is a poolside bar known as Leaping Horse Libations, a tribute to the diving horses that used to entertain Guests at Atlantic City's Steel Pier.

There is a clock shaped like Mickey's head behind the bar.

 A REAL TUFFY **Seashore Sweets':** I will warn you … this is an extremely difficult one to spot. Look closely at the sign that hangs above the entrance to this shop.

A faint Hidden Mickey is situated in the blue clouds between the legendary Sweets' sisters that inspired the shop's confectionary collection.

DISNEY'S POP CENTURY RESORT

 Everything POP Shopping & Dining: Inside this store, Hidden Mickey images pop up throughout the place.

Images of Mickey abound, appearing on light fixtures, makeshift ovens, and microwaves, plus even the store's product display racks.

A REAL TUFFY **Everything POP Shopping & Dining:** Once inside the food court area, look out for a tiny black Hidden Mickey shape.

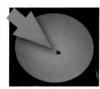

Look for it in one of the light fixtures in the food court area. Interestingly, the Hidden Mickey shape appears in a variety of light fixtures depending on the day!

 Everything POP Shopping & Dining: This time, look down at the tile floor of the food court area.

There you will discover four Hidden Mickey shapes etched in the tile work at different locations within the food court area.

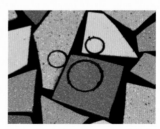

 Main lobby: Located on the back wall of the main building, across from the registration desk, is a collection of shadow box cases featuring pop-culture references from throughout the years.

In the 1950s case, there is a reference to Disneyland and the Mickey Mouse Club television show. The 1970s case has a reference to the opening of the Walt Disney World Resort.

👍 **Main lobby:** In the same location across from the registration desk, there is a children's area to keep the kids entertained while the adults go through the check-in process.

To the right of the television, there is a fish bowl painted on the wall. A Hidden Mickey is formed by the bubbles coming from a fish's mouth.

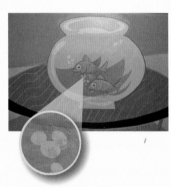

☝ **1960s building exterior:** A large display of Mowgli and Baloo from *The Jungle Book* dominates the facade of this building, located just past the Hippy Dippy Pool.

On the building wall behind Mowgli, seek out a delicately etched Hidden Mickey among the green leaves that are near the brown tree.

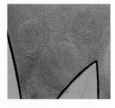

☝ **1970s building exterior:** While not hidden, and oh-so-larger than life, this Mickey is a spot-on ringer.

The thirty-foot-high Mickey phone serves as one of the icons of the building.

👍 **1980s building exterior:** Located on the personal computer that serves as this building's icon are Mickey designs and shapes, which are featured all over the computer.

Mickeys can be found on the screen and keyboard of the computer.

A REAL TUFFY **1980s building exterior:** This structure also has a large figure of Roger Rabbit standing on top of a barrel. On the mural directly behind Roger Rabbit is a mural featuring plants and bushes.

Look for a classic Hidden Mickey shape in one of the bushes on the very bottom right portion of the mural.

✌ **On the grounds:** Three overlapping rings form the shape of Mickey outside the main lobby of the resort and heading toward the bus stop.

They can be found at the end of each guardrail you pass on your journey to pick up a Walt Disney World Transportation bus.

DISNEY'S ART OF ANIMATION RESORT

👉 **Hallways:** There are several hallway carpets throughout each of the resort's buildings that feature Hidden Mickey shapes.

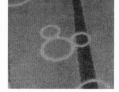

A great example is a white bubble outline on a blue patterned rug.

👆 **Ink & Paint Shop:** Once inside this store, find a sign that reads, **PACKAGE PICK-UP**.

Then look directly under the sign and you will discover a three-dimensional Mickey Mouse standing there.

👉 **Landscape of Flavors:** Several Hidden Mickey images can be found as you comb through this dining facility. *The Lion King* section, for example, features a beautiful mural that serves as the light cover.

On the light cover, there is moss that forms a perfect Hidden Mickey on the side of one of the trees.

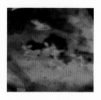

 Landscape of Flavors: In *The Little Mermaid* themed room of the food court area, there is a light cover and mural featuring Ariel's grotto.

230

If you look closely, you may catch a glimpse of Mickey Mouse that's cleverly hidden in a picture frame among Ariel's human artifacts.

👉 **Landscape of Flavors:** There are banners that cascade down from the food court area in the *Finding Nemo* section. They are designed to represent the EAC, or the East Australian Current, as depicted in the animated feature.

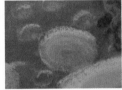

Look for the jellyfish on the banners that strategically form Hidden Mickey shapes.

👍 **Main lobby:** Seek out the grouping of colorful benches that dominate this resort's main building.

The benches are opposite the check-in counter for the resort; they have classic Hidden Mickey patterns in them.

👉 **Pool:** At the two ends of the *Finding Nemo* pool area, locate a green fish in each area with a smiling face. They are similar.

On the backside of each fish is a classic Hidden Mickey.

DISNEY'S ANIMAL KINGDOM RESORT AREA

With the introduction of Disney's Animal Kingdom Resort area, a new breed of Disney resorts was born. The All-Star collection of resorts brought a new and efficient brand of resort to this corner of the world. Another unique addition to this resort area was Disney's Coronado Springs Resort, which focused on the business traveler, offering convention space and accommodation never before seen on the property. Finally, with the opening of Disney's Animal Kingdom Lodge, the region offered accommodations tied very skillfully into the fabric of the theme park that shares its name.

DISNEY'S ALL-STAR SPORTS RESORT

👉 **End Zone Food Court:** Located inside the seating area are pictures that fill the walls of the dining facility.

A closer look will reveal a few Hidden Mickey images tucked away in some of the pictures.

👆 **On the grounds:** If you venture out and beyond the main building of the resort and past the main swimming pool, there is a Mickey Mouse statue.

The statue itself stands directly above a classic Hidden Mickey, who's equipped with black ears (that rest on a white head), embedded in the cement.

👉 **Sport Goofy Gifts:** Hidden Mickey designs reside all over the carpet in this shop.

The head of each Mickey is represented by the baseballs that decorate the carpet.

DISNEY'S ALL-STAR MUSIC RESORT

👉 **Country Fair building exterior:** A collection of bolos hang off the side of this building. Located on these shoestring neckties are Mickey designs.

While rather large and not so hidden, the blue coloring that blends into the background makes them a bit less obvious.

👍 **Country Fair building exterior:** It is fair to say these boots were made for walking, but only if your shoe size is a 270!

While you take a gander at these incredible huge boots, peer at the front and back of the shoe and discover a classic Hidden Mickey.

✌️ **Intermission Food Court:** In the seating area of this dining destination, there are many pictures on the walls.

Look closely and you may find Mickey hiding in some of the pictures.

Jazz Inn courtyard: While frequenting this jazzy courtyard, seek out a classic Hidden Mickey, which can be found atop the large cymbal stand.

The Mouse ears are disguised as wing nuts on these colossal-sized musical instruments.

☞ **Main lobby:** When in this area, which is better known as Melody Hall, look behind the check-in counter. There is a mural that runs the length of the counter.

On the far-left side of the mural is a group of Latin music–inspired dancers. A close look at the woman and her dress will reveal a Hidden Mickey in the design.

DISNEY'S ALL-STAR MOVIES RESORT

 Donald's Double Feature: Stare up at the high shelf in this store, and you will discover a collection of film reels.

On the front of these film reels are classic Hidden Mickeys.

👍 **Main lobby:** This area of the resort features a mural that runs the length of the check-in counter. Look carefully—a collection of Hidden Mickeys are strategically placed in the mural.

The first is on the right-hand side of the mural, and it features a theater named the Los Angeles. On the far-left marquee, running up the side of the building, is your first Hidden Mickey head.

A REAL TUFFY *The second is an amphitheater with two California palm trees on each side of the upper building, which forms a set of Mouse ears.*

The third and fourth Hidden Mickeys are found in the tree line in front of each building previously mentioned: the Los Angeles theater and the amphitheater; the trees form a classic Hidden Mickey.

👆 **Toy Story building exterior:** You may be tempted to play a game with this checker set located in this part of the resort.

But, before you attempt to do so, check out the Hidden Mickey designs featured on top of each game piece.

237

DISNEY'S CORONADO SPRINGS RESORT

 Buildings: In the Ranchos section of the resort, heading toward Building 6, near a small bridge, there is a collection of flat, gray rocks.

A closer look at some of these rocks reveals a classic Hidden Mickey.

 Buildings: To the right of these rocks are numerous sand-colored rocks.

There, too, are three large rocks that form a traditional Hidden Mickey design.

 Bus stops: Any sign of Mickey around here?

There is a side profile of Mickey Mouse sitting comfortably in a bus on some of the bus stop signs scattered throughout the resort.

A REAL TUFFY **Convention Center lobby:** Just outside the restrooms for the Convention Center, look for a themed painting featuring a collection of Hidden Mickey shapes.

The cobblestone road in the painting provides a few perfectly positioned circles.

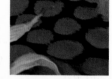

 Convention Center lobby: In the main atrium of the Convention Center, chandeliers run the length of the hallway.

There are classic Hidden Mickey shapes featured on the inner and outer sides of these chandeliers.

👍 **Convention Center, Veracruz Exhibit Hall:** Try to find similar Hidden Mickey patterns in this hall's light fixtures.

This time they are square lights attached to the ceiling.

✋ **Entrance:** There is a set of two large wooden-like doors that mark the entrance to the resort.

A Mickey face can be found as a three-dimensional medallion on the outside of the door. Interestingly, there is a similar set of doors at the back end of the resort's building, directly across the entrance; and there, too, is a Mickey face medallion.

A REAL TUFFY **Main lobby:** On the far wall here, there is a coat of arms depicting Disney's Coronado Springs Resort. Situated perfectly against this wall are three floodlights illuminating the logo and wall.

The three floodlights shine and form a classic Mickey head. The best way to view this Hidden

Mickey is to stand at the other end of the hallway, which provides you with the best possible vantage point.

👉 **Main lobby:** Once inside the main building of the resort, head down the path toward the Pepper Market Food Court. Prior to arriving at this colorfully

themed food court area, there is a lounge known as Rix.

On the back exterior wall of Rix are beautifully styled black circles that form classic Hidden Mickeys.

 Marina: Take a short stroll from the main building of the resort, and head toward the marina. Stop in front of a lamppost directly opposite the rentals location; your next Hidden Mickey is about to be revealed.

Look down at the cement and you will discover a Hidden Mickey etched in the pathway.

Marina: Continue to the marina dock and find a wooden plank near the water with a familiar-shaped knothole.

> *The plank is near a metal cleat and features three intentional-seeming circles that form a classic Hidden Mickey.*

Pool: The Dig Site is one of the Walt Disney World Resort's best themed pool areas, representing a lost Mayan kingdom that's been uncovered during an archeological dig. At the entrance, across the lagoon directly opposite the main building, are two rock columns marking one of the openings to this site.

> *On the right toward the very top portion of the wall is a Mickey-shaped relief etched in the rock.*

Pool: As you exit the pool area, on the opposite side of the two columns, again on your right, there is a similar Hidden Mickey etched in the wall.

> *This Mickey is in the furthest left portion, on the corner.*

Pool: Near the restrooms of the pool area hanging on the wall is a representation of a Mayan calendar.

> *If you look closely at the one corner of the calendar, you'll spot a classic Hidden Mickey shape.*

DISNEY'S ANIMAL KINGDOM LODGE-JAMBO HOUSE

 Boma—Flavors of Africa: There are three classic Hidden Mickeys inside the restaurant. The first is on the far-right wall, near the entrance.

There is an impression of Mickey embedded in the wall. It is near the top of the wall, and it is a classic Mickey head.

Boma—Flavors of Africa: There are also several chair designs that are featured throughout the restaurant.

The high-back chairs in Boma highlight everyone's favorite mouse.

Boma—Flavors of Africa: And finally, even though this Hidden Mickey is not depicted on a permanent structure, it can be seen each day.

Located at the sweets table of the buffet are three trays of cookies that Guests can enjoy during every serving. Plus, all three trays form a classic Mickey: it's comprised of one large tray and two smaller ones.

Entrance: The resort is just bursting with hidden images of Mickey. Look for this Mickey not wanting to wait for his place inside the resort.

The Hidden Mickey is located on the second landing outside of the Jambo House to the left of the porte cochere. It is on one of the faces of the ceremonial figures marking the resort's facade.

Entrance: Between the two sets of entrance doors on the right sidewall is a mural featuring a lizard.

One of the spots on the lizard is a classic Hidden Mickey. It's on the creature's back.

Hallways: Classic Hidden Mickey designs are found in the Guest hallway carpets throughout the resort.

Notice rectangles encasing three Mickeys each, in alternating directions.

A REAL TUFFY **Hallways:** Look for this very unique elevator near the Fitness Center if you wish to pursue your Hidden Mickey quest.

There is an elevator located near the Fitness Center that features a wooden cutout of a Mickey head in the right corner of the elevator. The Hidden Mickey is just below the control panel and buttons for the elevator.

Jiko—The Cooking Place: There are two classic Hidden Mickey designs that call this restaurant home. The first is found on the ceiling of the restaurant.

It is formed by two large orange oven exhaust columns and one white column. The three, when placed together, form a Hidden Mickey.

Jiko—The Cooking Place: The restaurant also features a beautiful scenic glass window.

Outside the window, there is a shallow pool area with a Hidden Mickey sculpted on the first rock island on the left.

Main lobby: Peruse the columns that surround this main area of the resort.

At the base of these columns are three logs, which are tied together. Each one forms an upside-down Hidden Mickey.

Main lobby: Once you discover those columns, follow them up toward the ceiling. At the top of these pillars are African-themed shields featuring three black circles.

While not a perfect Hidden Mickey proportionally, the sight is reminiscent of the mouse's signature silhouette.

A REAL TUFFY **Main lobby:** There is a beautiful staircase that takes Guests to the entrance of Boma restaurant. Once you reach the first landing, there is a small waterfall on your right.

Tucked away in the rockwork of the waterfall is a classic Hidden Mickey.

Mara: Inside this quick-service facility are two classic Hidden Mickey shapes.

On the side ceiling near the food area is an impression of Mickey in a collection of leaves.

Mara: There is also a Hidden Mickey shape that can be found on the back wall mural of the restaurant.

Mickey is found on the monkey, which is climbing a tree in the middle of the mural.

Victoria Falls lounge: Mickey is rocking in this lobby bar and lounge area!

Look for a three-circle Mickey carved into the rockwork by the falls.

A REAL TUFFY **Viewing area:** A walk down the back staircase of the resort leads you to the outside part of the resort, home to the savannah viewing area. Prior to reaching the overlook, there is a large vine-inspired column.

About three quarters up the vine-covered column, on the left-hand side, there is a clever Hidden Mickey within the flora.

Viewing area: On the left side of the viewing area, look for the rock design of a mother giraffe and her young calf for your next Hidden Mickey.

Three spots on the mother giraffe form a perfect Hidden Mickey.

Viewing area: For almost ninety years Mickey Mouse has made an impression on the old and young alike. Mickey also makes a nice impression of his head on the side of Arusha Rock in the resort's viewing area.

Locate light brown crates situated between a trash can and a green bush and then look upward to see the imprint.

DISNEY'S ANIMAL KINGDOM LODGE-KIDANI VILLAGE

👉 **Main lobby:** As soon as you enter the lobby, stop by the themed clock on a table.

If you look between the six and seven, you'll see there is a Hidden Mickey on the clock.

A REAL TUFFY **Main lobby:** There are several African-themed chandeliers in this area of the resort.

On the one located in the middle, closest to the registration desk, there is an image of a ladybug that's designed to represent a Hidden Mickey.

👍 **Sanaa:** At the check-in desk of this restaurant, look to the left of the counter.

Discover a Hidden Mickey formed by three hanging baskets.

🖐 **Sanaa:** On the wall of one of the large seating areas in the restaurant are three themed plates and basket-ware that merge to form the shape of Mickey.

The Mickey is framed by three large wooden spoons on each side.

👉 **Sanaa:** While still in the restaurant, peer down at the tabletops to catch a classic Hidden Mickey design.

Mickey is at the center of an ornately patterned circle.

👍 **Viewing area:** As you head back in from the savannah viewing deck, look for this classic Hidden Mickey, which is situated in the rocks you pass once you walk back into the resort.

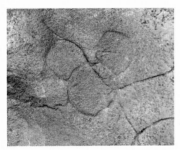

The Mickey is centered about midway between the top and bottom of the rock formation.

DISNEY SPRINGS RESORT AREA

For Guests wishing to make a more substantial investment in their future Walt Disney World vacations, the establishments of the Disney Springs Resort area are ideal. In 1991, the Disney Vacation Club was introduced, offering Guests the opportunity to partake in the vacation ownership experience. The first resort to open featuring this unique opportunity was Disney's Old Key West Resort. Later additions to the Disney Springs Resort area included a collection of uniquely themed resort properties such as Disney's Port Orleans Riverside and French Quarter resorts, and Disney's Saratoga Springs Resort.

DISNEY'S SARATOGA SPRINGS RESORT & SPA

👉 **The Artist's Palette:** There is an impression of Mickey on the door handle of the restaurant.

It is located down the hallway heading toward The Turf Club Bar and Grill on the right-hand side hallway. It is of Mickey swinging a golf club.

👉 **The Artist's Palette/The Turf Club Bar and Grill:** Look for a collection of surreal-looking Mickey shapes on the gate leading from The Artist's Palette to The Turf Club Bar and Grill.

Mickey is depicted in blue and white shapes throughout the gate.

👉 **Disney Vacation Club Preview Center:** Located in the Welcome Center is a large rotunda featuring a 360-degree mural of Disney Vacation Club destinations throughout the world.

Look for an entrance marquee for Disney's Animal Kingdom, a Disney Cruise Line ship, a gold tree next to Cinderella Castle, and other Mickey references.

👉 **Disney Vacation Club Preview Center:** In 1958, Norman Rockwell created one of his most famous paintings, *The Runaway*, for *The Saturday Evening Post*. There is now a picture that pays tribute to that famous painting located in the Disney Vacation Club

Farewell Lobby. But instead of a police officer, as featured in the original portrait, a Disney-costumed train conductor has been inserted in his place.

In the picture, which is on the wall of the small ice cream parlor, there is an old-fashioned radio with everyone's favorite mouse on the front.

Disney Vacation Club Preview Center: The Farewell Lobby also boasts a beautiful mural of clouds above the seating area of the small ice cream parlor.

A quick look at the mural will reveal Mickey Mouse, Donald, and Goofy as clouds.

Grandstand Pool: Head to this themed pool area for two Hidden Mickey shapes. The first is located on a gate, and it can be spotted best as you leave the pool area.

The white gate features an almost complete Mickey head cutout.

Grandstand Pool: The second Hidden Mickey is located at the Backstretch Pool Bar. The tiny Hidden Mickey can be found on the wall of the pool bar underneath the counter.

Look for a mural and a grouping of trees. There is a Hidden Mickey pattern that can be found in the tree line.

☞ **Main entrance:** Featured at the entrance of the resort is a jockey atop a horse in a winner's circle. Draped across the horse and the jockey is a blanket of roses.

A REAL TUFFY *If you look very carefully at the bottom portion of the roses, you will discover an intricately carved Hidden Mickey among the roses. The Hidden Mickey is actually featured similarly on both sides of the rose blanket.*

On that same jockey, look at the back and front of his jacket and you will discover images of Mickey's head featured as the logo.

The horse's bridle also features three rings designed to resemble a Hidden Mickey.

👍 **On the grounds:** Mickey makes some clever appearances in several areas on or near the property's buildings.

Located on many of the buildings are Hidden Mickey heads, which have been inserted throughout the lattice and railings.

Attached to the upper corners of most of the building entrances of this resort are porch and outside lights with Hidden Mickey designs patterned into them.

Mickey adorns the tops of some building towers.

Look for obelisks in and around the resort. At the base of these structures are perfectly shaped Mickey heads.

The Turf Club Bar and Grill: Look for a collection of shadow boxes inside the restuarant.

Two of the frames encase equestrian equipment. Classic Hidden Mickey designs can be found in each of these frames.

The Turf Club Bar and Grill: In the hallway leading into this restaurant, Guests should take in the display cabinets, which each contain a jockey's jacket.

If you can spot the pink jacket, you will certainly discover another collection of Hidden Mickey designs.

The Turf Club Bar and Grill: Once you enter the restaurant, look on the wall to your left. You will discover a set of billiard balls in a shadow box frame.

The billiard balls feature images of some of your classic Disney characters.

DISNEY'S OLD KEY WEST RESORT

👆 **Conch Flats General Store:** Look for Hidden Mickey shapes throughout the fence's woodwork and at the bottom of the stands inside the shop.

The ears are perfectly shaped on these designs, but the head is cut off about two-thirds the way down the fence.

👆 **Main lobby/On the grounds:** The registration desk is located in the Hospitality House, which is set along a themed dockside landing containing the fitness center, arcade, food locations, and more. As you approach the check-in counter, look past the desk and spot classic Hidden Mickey designs on the fence railing against the back wall.

Those same Hidden Mickey shapes can also be found on the railings of Guest buildings throughout the resort, as well as various buildings around the Hospitality House complex.

👆 **Pool:** The resort's main pool area features a slide built into a giant sand castle-shaped structure.

After you've taken the plunge, look back at the mouth of the slide; it's shaped like Mickey's head.

DISNEY'S PORT ORLEANS RESORT-FRENCH QUARTER

Sassagoula Floatworks and Food Factory:
There is a classic upside-down Hidden Mickey inside the food court area.

It is made from white and blue gemstones, which decorate a crown that hangs from the ceiling of the food court seating area.

A REAL TUFFY Sassagoula Floatworks and Food Factory: While still in this location, look up to the rafters of the building to view the Mardi Gras-inspired sun.

A close look at the left eye of the sun will reveal a Hidden Mickey shape in the center of that eye.

DISNEY'S PORT ORLEANS RESORT-RIVERSIDE

👉 **Fulton's General Store:** Inside this store, a collection of canisters reside on a shelf that's adjacent to where customer merchandise is sold.

On each of the white canisters, which are marked with words such as FLOUR, SUGAR, and CEREAL, there are small blue-colored classic Mickey heads.

👍 **Main lobby:** Located above the registration area are classic Hidden Mickeys, which are repeated in the wooden latticework circling this particular section of the resort.

Each arch features three separate Mickey outlines.

👈 **Main lobby:** While you are still looking upward, concentrate on the large ceiling fans that dominate the registration area.

Featured on the side brackets of the large fans are classic Hidden Mickey designs.

There are also Hidden Mickey designs featured on the ends of the braces that suspend the large punkah fans from the ceiling.

👉 **Parterre Place exteriors:** Hidden Mickeys abound on the green-painted iron railings throughout the entire building.

Mickey appears on each rectangle-shaped piece of the building's ornate railing.

INDEX

For information address Disney Editions, 1101 Flower Street, Glendale, California 91201

Editorial Director: Wendy Lefkon
Editor: Jennifer Eastwood
Designer: H. Clark Wakabayashi
Design assistant: Chi Chi Wakabayashi

This book's producers would like to thank Jennifer Black, Monique Diman, Dennis Ely, Winnie Ho, Warren Meislin, Betsy Mercer, Scott Piehl, Steve Plotkin, Chip Poakeart, Michael Serrian, Betsy Singer, Muriel Tebid, Marybeth Tregarthen, Dushawn Ward, and Jessie Ward.

ISBN 978-1-4847-2778-2
FAC-008598-16134
Printed in the United States of America
First Paperback Edition, May 2016
10 9 8 7 6 5 4 3 2 1
Visit www.disneybooks.com

D23
The Official Disney Fan Club

Disney.com/D23

SUSTAINABLE FORESTRY INITIATIVE

Certified Chain of Custody
At Least 20% Certified Forest Content
www.sfiprogram.org
SFI-00993

For Text Only

READER'S FINDS

_____
_____
_____
_____
_____
_____
_____
_____
_____
_____
_____
_____
_____
_____
_____
_____
_____
_____
_____
_____
_____
_____
_____
_____
_____
_____
_____
_____